PETER ISLER'S
LITTLE BLUE BOOK OF
SAILING SECRETS

Peter Isler

WILEY
John Wiley & Sons, Inc.

Published by John Wiley & Sons, Inc., Hoboken, New Jersey
Published simultaneously in Canada

Designations used by companies to distinguish their products are often claimed as trademarks. In all instances where John Wiley & Sons, Inc., is aware of a claim, the product names appear in initial capital or ALL CAPITAL letters. Readers, however, should contact the appropriate companies for more complete information regarding trademarks and registration.

Limit of Liability/Disclaimer of Warranty: While the publisher and the author have used their best efforts in preparing this book, they make no representations or warranties with respect to the accuracy or completeness of the contents of this book and specifically disclaim any implied warranties of merchantability or fitness for a particular purpose. No warranty may be created or extended by sales representatives or written sales materials. The advice and strategies contained herein may not be suitable for your situation. You should consult with a professional where appropriate. Neither the publisher nor the author shall be liable for any loss of profit or any other commercial damages, including but not limited to special, incidental, consequential, or other damages.

For general information about our other products and services, please contact our Customer Care Department within the United States at (800) 762-2974, outside the United States at (317) 572-3993 or fax (317) 572-4002.

Wiley also publishes its books in a variety of electronic formats. Some content that appears in print may not be available in electronic books. For more information about Wiley products, visit our web site at www.wiley.com.

Library of Congress Cataloging-in-Publication Data:

ISBN 978-0-470-90263-9 (cloth); ISBN 978-0-470-95087-6 (ebk.);
ISBN 978-0-470-95088-3 (ebk.); ISBN 978-0-470-95089-0 (ebk.)

Printed in the United States of America

10 9 8 7 6 5 4 3 2 1

Contents

The Sailing Life

Who would have thought that a baseball-playing kid from Cincinnati, Ohio, would end up making a career out of the sport of sailboat racing? The bookies in Vegas would have lengthened the odds greatly after my first day at junior sailing class, when, sitting in a dinghy drifting backward with the sail luffing—fully embarrassed—my sailing instructor came over in his motorboat and said with a sneer at me, "You really *don't* know how to sail, do you?" There was certainly a good measure of happenstance involved, but the bottom line is that I loved sailing from the moment I first tried it.

Emerging from college, I pursued a calling that was far from the typical career paths of my peers at Yale, many of whom became lawyers, doctors, investment bankers, and corporate executives. I mounted an Olympic campaign, and then worked my way from boat to boat—regatta to regatta—in a manner that made it clear to those watching that I had never considered coming up with a "five-year plan." Some observers have probably thought of me as broad-reaching through life. So be it. I would not trade my life and experiences in the sport of sailing for all the baseballs made in China.

What was it that piqued my interest in the sport of sailboat racing? Even today, looking back, it's hard to pinpoint. As a child I'd always been drawn to the water, and there are some beautiful places on this planet that you can only see by boat. I suppose, too, that I possess a competitive streak (mellowed over the years) that racing helped satisfy. Another contributory factor may have been the intellectual challenge of racing a sailboat, and the opportunity to learn about a variety of disciplines (teamwork, aerodynamics, meteorology, physical fitness, and seamanship, to name a few) and apply those lessons in a competitive environment. I'm sure another dynamic in play was my fascination (and friendship) with the people involved in this game of harnessing the forces of Mother Nature to make their boat go a little faster (and in a more clever direction) than their competition.

Looking back on a career that has moved into its fourth decade, I can't help but be thankful that my mother moved my brother, sister, and me from Ohio to Connecticut when I was thirteen, thereby curtailing a baseball career that likely would have fizzled out long before it ever really got started, and opening up the door to a sport that I continue to learn about and grow with. My steps along the way all seemed clear enough at the time, but I was not following any well-trodden path. When I started sailing, a professional sailor was someone who worked on, maintained, or delivered boats or had a "real" job in the industry, that is, in sailmaking, boatbuilding, naval architecture, or a related profession. Today, a handful of us make a living racing boats. But even among that group, the variations on the theme are many.

My first sailing job was as an instructor at a junior sailing program at Noroton Yacht Club in Connecticut. As much as I loved to race, I found I also derived great pleasure in teaching racing and sailing to others. Over the years, I've taught clinics, given seminars, coached teams, written articles and books, and had countless informal dockside sessions spreading my knowledge of and love for the sport. At a fairly early point in my career, I decided that the sport of sailing had given me so much opportunity and pleasure that part of my life's quest would be to share this penchant and skill set with others.

After my first America's Cup victory (sailing with Dennis Conner and the *Stars & Stripes* team in Fremantle, Australia), that feeling of mission to help grow the sport of sailing strengthened. And in recent years, the opportunities for me to share the love have expanded, too—as an author, speaker, and even television announcer. And so we come to this book—an idea that took fruit in conversations with my friend Peter Economy as we discussed the deep wisdom and broad appeal of the classic golf book *Harvey Penick's Little Red Book*. "How about a book like Penick's, but about sailing?" asked Peter.

So herein the reader finds some of my experiences—the lessons I've learned from my life on a boat. Some of these are in the form of tips for racers, while others are broader principles of life that I discovered applied just as well in my sailing career. Some of my most unforgettable sea stories are in this book, and I've asked a few friends and fellow sailors who I greatly respect to share a salty tale or two of their own. In these short, bite-size chapters, my aim is to whet the appetite of someone who has never set foot in a sailboat, as well as to share some of my most treasured racing secrets with the inveterate sailor looking for an edge. My hope is that this book will in some measure be a match for Penick's in drawing newcomers further into the sport, and entertaining and enlightening those old salts who, like me, are already hooked.

So hoist your sails just as I've done for so many years, and keep learning because that's the one thing that I'm sure of about sailing—there's always more to learn!

⌒⌒⌒

Secrecy vs. Sharing

Although I can't now remember exactly when it happened, there was a day many years ago when I went from being someone who asked all the questions, to being someone whom fellow sailors came to for advice. It started innocuously enough—probably when a competitor wanted to find out how I played the wind shifts after I won a race at some collegiate regatta. Later, when I started sailing Olympic-class boats such as the 470 and the Soling, speed tricks—the "trade secrets" of the speed demons in these classes—were the most valued currency in the regatta parking lot.

In those days my heroes were guys such as Paul Elvström and Buddy Melges. Elvström—the "Great Dane"—won four gold medals in four different Olympiads, and he wrote books about how to win, sharing his philosophies and techniques with us mere mortals. When I got into the Soling class before the soon-to-be boycotted 1980 Olympics, I learned that Melges—the "Wizard of Zenda"—was as approachable as a small-town merchant. Buddy would drop what he was doing and answer any question asked of him, sharing his tips and techniques to make a Soling go fast. Now, this was the guy who won a gold medal in the Olympics with a string of bullets. Sure he was a sailmaker, but he'd help the guys who didn't buy his sails, too. Any subject was fair game.

Being exposed to these mentors helped me formulate my own attitude toward sharing knowledge with my competitors. I strongly believe it is both healthy and right to help others, especially when they reach out for information. My attitude is that if telling someone my "secrets" enables that person to beat me, then I need to work harder and sail better. I see sports as an opportunity for you to test yourself against a yardstick (your competition). And if you really care about honing your performance, you will want that yardstick to be as high as it can be.

In those early Olympic campaign days, some of my peers were quite secretive, keeping their technical knowledge and techniques behind the curtain. But that's a defensive position, not one that encourages growth. I'd rather be the guy trying to break new ground and developing new equipment (including sails, rigging systems, and underwater foils) than be the one trying to protect the status quo. Sailing is all about demonstrating excellence in a bunch of different disciplines, and being able to make swift decisions and then execute them in a very changeable environment. So no matter how much knowledge you have, or all the amazing equipment you have on your boat, you aren't going to be a great sailor until you can put everything together at just the right time, while all the conditions around you (wind, current, the trim of your boat, the position of your competitors) are constantly changing.

That's what it takes to win—not just having the fastest system to pull up the spinnaker, or whatever happens to be the latest gimmick du jour.

Of course, as you move up toward the America's Cup level of competition, there are secrets—very big ones—protected by ironclad contracts, nondisclosure agreements, security guards, and remote-control cameras. To an America's Cup team, the design and engineering of their boat are priceless intellectual properties not unlike the Coca-Cola Company's top-secret formula for Coke.

Having come to the AC game with my well-developed attitude that sharing and being open with the competition is healthy, I had and still have a hard time with all the secrecy surrounding the Cup. I understand that it's a necessary part of the game, but all this secrecy can be taken to an unhealthy extreme. I think most sailors would agree (although prob-ably not the designers and engineers), and that's why sailors so enjoy the offseason moments of an America's Cup cam-paign where, in exhibition regattas, the teams have more of a chance to interact. The boats they are sailing in these regattas are older-generation craft with few if any secrets left to hide. There are no fences separating the teams from one another or guards keeping spies out. It's more like a regular regatta.

Most of us grew up in this highly social sport of sailing, where competitors have to work together at some level to improve their sailing. When that part of the game is taken away, or changed, the game feels different.

$\backsim\!\backsim\!\backsim$

The Rules

As with any other sport (and in life in general), there are rules in sailing that you have to follow. They are called the *Racing Rules of Sailing* and they have a long history that goes back well over a hundred years. Break the rules, and you are liable to be penalized in that race or even thrown out of the competition. In my experience, the smartest thing anyone competing in any sport can do is to know the rules as well as or better than anyone else. This means being better versed than your competitors whenever possible. But if you want to win at the highest level, your rules knowledge should meet or exceed that of the judges or umpires. A secret to success is often pushing your on-the-water performance or the equipment and setup of your boat right up to the line that divides what is allowed under the rules from what is prohibited—without actually crossing it. Now, to take your boat and its equipment to this line and not beyond requires an intimate knowledge of the rules. To be able to make split-second tactical decisions in crowded, fast-changing situations, a solid grasp of the rules is invaluable. Indeed, the foundation of all sailing tactics—the boat-for-boat strategic battle—is in the racing rules.

The sport of sailboat racing is governed internationally by the International Sailing Federation (ISAF: www.sailing.org). The ISAF updates the *Racing Rules of Sailing* every four years (updates go into effect the January after the Summer

Olympiad). Here, in condensed and creatively edited verbiage, are five of the most basic right-of-way rules that almost every racing sailor has learned. But using the rules to the greatest advantage in your racing requires that you go beyond the first step of knowledge (where many sailors stop) and learn all the right-of-way rules. They only occupy a small part of the rule book, but you should know them better than you know your own phone number.

- Avoid collisions with other boats and any turning marks.
- A starboard-tack boat (with the wind blowing on its right side) has right of way over a port-tack boat.
- For boats on the same tack, the leeward (more down-wind, or farther from the wind) boat has the right of way over the windward (more upwind, or closer to the wind) boat.
- For boats on the same tack, the overtaking boat must keep clear of the boat it is passing.
- When rounding marks, the inside boat has the right of way.

Being on top of the rules is so important that America's Cup teams have full-time rules advisors who help the sailors refine their match-racing tactics and even represent their team in protest hearings. These same advisors (or other legal experts) help the teams analyze the Cup's design and construction rules to identify loopholes of opportunity and to ensure that the team's equipment is (just) on the right side of the law.

I'm not suggesting that you must take a similar "sea-lawyerly" approach to your sailing (unless you are planning to mount an America's Cup campaign). In fact, I find such overt use of the rules and flaunting one's knowledge rather uncool. And didn't Shakespeare write about the failings of a guy who "complaineth too much"? Remember, what goes 'round, comes 'round. If you get known as a protest-happy sea lawyer on the water, your competitors will be less likely to give you a break when they have the opportunity. And believe me, in sailing it doesn't hurt to have a friend or two out there to wave you across in a tight crossing when you are the give-way port tack boat. Really understanding the right-of-way rules doesn't mean you will protest every time you can. It means that you use this knowledge to be more confident in your tight, boat-on-boat tactics, and you will actually lower the odds that you'll end up in a post-race protest hearing. The latter point is significant because any time you go into a pro-test hearing—no matter how strong you feel your case is—there is a very real possibility that you will come out the loser.

Keeping It Real

Sailing can be very serious business. When someone sinks millions of dollars into a boat and a team to try to win a race, you *know* he is serious. But I also know that no matter how important your endeavor, when you have some fun along the way, you end up doing better in the long run.

It's like when you're in school. The boring, "serious" classes and lectures just seem to go on and on and on forever. You can't wait to get out. But when you've got a good teacher—one who knows how to entertain and make the subject fun—the time goes by far too quickly. And guess what? You end up learning more when you're having fun. During my undergraduate years at Yale, I enjoyed learning from some of the most inspiring lec-turers in the world, and my appreciation and retention of the course material soared. But I also had several classes with some real duds. They knew their stuff, but they had no charisma and their teaching style was . . . turgid, to be kind. Needless to say, it took a lot more effort to soak in the material in those classes.

The two guys who have been at the helm of more America's Cup winners than anyone alive today, Dennis Conner and Russell Coutts, are great examples of people who, in the heat of battle, can make a joke and break the tension as a way to keep everybody balanced. Sure, they are inspiring and demanding to sail with, but their leadership style is relaxed, confident, and, quite frankly . . . fun. And Tom Whidden, who has won the America's Cup three times and grew North Sails into *the* global powerhouse of the sailmaking industry, is a master of the practical joke—he knows just the right time to play his cards, and he plays them very well.

When we were in Fremantle practicing for the America's Cup, we needed someone to fill in and trim the jib sheet—the guy assigned to the trimmer position was off taking pictures of the sail or something. Trimming the jib sheet requires quick hands and good technique that takes some time to master. On a 12 Meter circa 1987, the jib sheets (the lines controlling the corner of the jib) were thick metal wires—5/16"-diameter cable, each bearing thousands of pounds of load—that could bite you pretty badly if you made a mistake. When the boat is tacked the trimmer has to quickly wrap this cable around the winch drum with several full revolutions, before it takes up full load and gets ripped out of his hands. And as the tension increases on the wire, the trimmer needs to have a smooth technique to add additional wraps on the winch drum quickly, but precisely to prevent the wire from getting tangled. Doing it right requires rock-solid nerves and no small amount of finesse.

The head of our technical team, a friend named Robert Hopkins—who has done a lot of sailing—happened to be on board that day and said, "Oh, I've done this before. I trimmed for a while with the British team." So he stepped in for our trimmer, moving to the windward trimmer position next to the winch drum.

We were about to go into a tack and Tom turned to me and said, "Watch this."

Robert was in position, facing forward, getting ready for the tacking maneuver. During the tack he would have to pull in maybe 50 feet of jib sheet wire and quickly wrap it around a winch as it loaded up with several tons of force. The jib sheet system is designed so that the wire leads from a nearby turning block to the winch drum at the perfect angle so that the wraps start at the bottom of the drum and then spiral upward like a spool of thread. If some slack gets into the system, the "perfect" lead is compromised, and the wire can easily tangle, wrapping on itself. This is called an override—it's like a gigantic knot preventing the sail from being trimmed in. When this happens, it becomes a major problem for the crew and usually causes the boat to slow down. The risk of an override is greatest in the very middle of the tacking maneuver, especially if the sail trimmer is a bit sloppy in adding those wraps. Not good if you want to win a race (or keep your job).

So we went into the tack, and Robert started wrapping the drum and pulling the sheet in. Right at that moment, Tom reached forward, out of Robert's line of vision, with a metal pole—a hydraulic handle. He flicked the jib sheet wire up, causing it to lead onto the drum from the top down instead of the bottom up. This triggered the heavy jib sheet wire to immediately wrap into a huge tangled mess and the tack had to be aborted. The entire crew (who had grown used to perfect tacks) turned to look at what had gone wrong and to see who had done it. Robert was red-faced—he had just tried his first tack as a jib trimmer in years, and he screwed it up. He turned around to tell Dennis how sorry he was that he messed up, and there were Tom, Dennis, and the rest of us just laughing away. Everyone on board had a good laugh—including Robert when he realized that Tom had set him up—and we carried on with our practice.

The late Roy Disney—former vice chairman of the Walt Disney Company—was a highly accomplished sailor with numerous ocean racing records to his credit. He was a great guy to sail with, and I enjoyed every one of the many miles I spent on the water with him and his team. During the two decades from the late 1980s to the late 2000s Roy headed one of the most successful ocean-racing teams in the world. Aboard a series of custom 70-to-90-foot sloops (Roy's boats—always named *Pyewacket*, after a cat in the 1958 film *Bell, Book and Candle*—kept getting bigger every time he built a new one), Roy and his team dominated ocean races—first on their home waters of the West Coast and then around the world. Once, during a shore-side conversation about his team's success, Roy told me about the importance of having fun when you're racing, even when you've put a lot of money on the line:

> A big part of it for me is we laugh a lot. We keep a certain amount of perspective about how important all this really is to the bigger picture. If you blew something, fine, you blew something—now let's go and you can make up for it. But you've got to have fun. I've always said, "The minute it's not fun, why should I do it?" Everybody seems to understand that. There are plenty of times to get serious.

~~~

The Fine Art of Jury-Rigging

There comes a time in every sailor's life when something breaks on board. Unfortunately, instead of happening when your boat is safely parked at dock or in your driveway, these breakdowns usually seem to occur when you're in the middle of a big race or far offshore and unable to get immediate help. Enter the fine art of jury-rigging—making temporary fixes to broken gear. The point is not to make it pretty, but to make it work—at least long enough to get you to safety or back in the race.

Because a race boat carries only limited spare parts and tools (varying by the size of the boat and the length of the race), jury-rigging requires a certain amount of creativity—sort of like that guy MacGyver in the television series of the same name. Here are some jury-rig essentials that every sailor should keep on board and easily accessible:

- **A sharp knife** This is one essential tool for most every sailing need—from cutting a heavily loaded rope to fending off Jaws.
- **Duct tape** It's amazing the sheer variety of things you can fix with duct tape. Get good-quality tape, not the cheap stuff.
- **Sticky-back** Also known as insignia cloth, this material is available from a sail loft and can be used to temporarily patch together tears and fix holes in sails and even boat hulls.
- **Rope** Always keep some extra rope around. It's amazing what you can do with some small-diameter (say 4 mm), high-strength (Spectra is a good choice) rope. This thin rope is easy to work with and to cut and tie knots in. And if you need to reattach two highly loaded parts, you can lace multiple loops and it will be as strong as much thicker rope.
- **Miscellaneous parts and tools** This depends on the size of your boat. A two-person Olympic 470 might

carry a Ziploc bag with the aforementioned supplies and a Leatherman-style multitool. On a larger boat, be sure you've got a few extra shackles, blocks, and fasteners in case parts break on your boat. And since even MacGyver needed a tool or two, throw an adjustable wrench, Vice-Grips, screwdrivers, wire cutters, hacksaw, hammer, sailmaker's sewing needles, Dacron thread, and a palm into a toolbox, too.

During our Soling Olympic campaign, Dave Perry, Tucker Edmundson, and I were racing in a big regatta—the Pre-Trials off the coast of Newport, Rhode Island—and as we sailed off the starting line in about 18 knots of wind, the pulley that held the mainsheet in the cockpit went flying. Its attaching shackle had blown to bits. (I guess I should mention here the importance of preventive maintenance to avoid the need to jury-rig things.) We were leading the series, and with the mainsail now luffing, we started to fall back from the fleet. My middleman, Dave Perry, pulled in the mainsheet from the boom and got the sail working again, but we needed to fix that pulley so we could trim the main effectively around the race course. Plus on that windy day, we needed Dave's weight hiked out over the side—not inboard holding the mainsheet near the boom.

I remembered a trick that my friend Tyler Keys had taught me on a big boat—how to make a temporary sheet stopper. I quickly asked for the rusty pair of Vice-Grip locking pliers that we kept on board, and adjusted the grip so it fit the diameter of the mainsheet. I then clamped it on the mainsheet where it was leading out of the pulley on the boom going down to Dave's hand. That took the load off the tail of the sheet so that Dave and Tucker could find a spare shackle and pin and easily reattach the errant mainsheet block. We were back in business in a couple of minutes—all three of us hiking out over the side. And all thanks to those rusty Vice-Grips!

Head Games

Like most athletes, I've been in some pressure-cooker situations where your thoughts and emotions play a critical role in your performance. One of the things I've learned through the science of sport psychology is to use the routine of your daily activities in sport to help keep you in the moment, especially as the stakes get bigger.

Even though you're sailing in the most important race of your life, you're still going to go into the locker room and get dressed the same way as you do every day you sail. You and your team are going to go through the same pre-sail preparation routine, the same process of leaving the dock. You still have to hoist the mainsail, and do the same pre-race sailing to check out the wind—just like on any other race day. It's okay to be nervous, but use your everyday race preparation routine as an anchor to help prevent that nervousness from overwhelming your mind. It might help to remind yourself that this is just another day on the water and you have to follow the same steps that you always follow on your way to the starting line.

It's natural to be excited, but it is important not to let your emotion or excitement—the "arousal level," as they call it in sport psychology—get out of control and hurt your performance. But that doesn't mean you can't be happy/sad and show emotion. Both can peacefully coexist as long as you are in control!

Sailing between a Reef and a Hard Place

My first America's Cup experience was as skipper for the *Courageous Challenge* in the 12 Meter World Championships preceding the 1987 America's Cup in Western Australia. I was young, and totally inexperienced at the helm of such a big boat. But I had a lot of notoriety as an up-and-coming, small-boat sailor and college-sailing champion—with a little bit of ocean racing experience—and I somehow got the job as skipper.

My crew and I flew down to Perth, Western Australia, in 1986, a month before the start of the Worlds. The team's owner was an inventor and philanthropist named Leonard Greene, and he had fitted Ted Turner's thirteen-year-old Cup winner *Courageous* with a winged keel. Western Australia in the summer, as we soon learned, is an incredibly windy place. On virtually every summer afternoon a strong sea breeze called the "Fremantle Doctor" comes onshore, building up to 25 knots.

I had a great crew with me. I had inherited some of the guys from the previous crew, but I made some additions, bringing in some really good one-design sailors and Olympic sailors—guys I knew and respected, but none of whom had any America's Cup experience, either. So as a whole, our crew was relatively green when it came to sailing the fabled *Courageous*, a big, powerful, 68-foot "lead mine" of a boat.

Late one afternoon, after a long practice session sailing in the Doctor, we discovered that the mainsail was stuck up at the top of the mast—we couldn't lower it. Aside from the immediate problem of having a stuck sail, there was one more problem: there was no way we could come into the harbor and back to the dock with our sail up—not when it was blowing 25 knots.

We needed to send a guy up the mast to see why the sail was stuck, and we were already a good hour's sail from the dock. But to sail back toward the harbor, we would have to sail upwind into the steep waves and bash along for miles and miles. The mast on a 12 Meter America's Cup boat is about 90 feet tall, and there's no way a person is going to survive the beating they would suffer at the top while sailing upwind through the nasty waves kicked up by the Doctor—there's no way he could even hang on.

So we had to turn downwind, away from the harbor, late in the afternoon on this extremely windy day. My friend, bowman Pat Dore, went to the top of the mast and ascertained that there was no way to lower the mainsail normally. The only way we were going to get it down was by popping the steel pin that was holding it into the fitting at the top of the mast. This mainsail headboard fitting—which normally slides up and down—was hopelessly stuck.

We hoisted a big hammer up to Pat and he worked on it for thirty minutes or so. By this time we're another five miles downwind. At the same time our navigator informed me that we were headed straight toward a reef.

With the reef approaching, time was short before we would have to turn back upwind with the mainsail still stuck. It was time for extreme measures, so we sent up a hacksaw, and Pat commenced sawing through the top of the mainsail.

Grand Prix mainsails weren't made of carbon fiber back then—they were made of Kevlar, the same ultratough stuff used in bulletproof vests. The sail was a tight weave of Kevlar, just like the sidewall of your tire. To ask a man at the top of a 90-foot mast swinging around in big waves to cut through this steel-like mesh with a simple hacksaw was a big request. But we had no other choice.

So Pat began sawing through the head of the mainsail, and we were quickly moving closer to the reef. It was a long process. He finally cut through the sail (leaving the stuck fitting and the very top of the mainsail at the top of the mast) and we were able to drop the mainsail, which was now totally destroyed. It was a brand-new sail that cost about fifty thousand dollars. After we returned to shore and I was able to talk to some of the guys who had more experience on the 12 Meters, I found out that there were some things we could have done to try to avoid destroying that sail. But being neophytes in big boats, we didn't have the knowledge that could have averted our close brush with disaster on the reef, and the loss of a very expensive sail.

While the loss of the sail was costly, I learned some valuable lessons in the process.

I learned that you shouldn't go out in conditions—or in equipment—that you're not prepared to handle. You should always have at least one experienced person on board in the event that things go wrong. He doesn't need to be the skipper and he doesn't need to be the decision maker on the boat. But even if you are the leader, you have to be willing to find and take that experienced advice when times get tough. In fact, as I learned later in my sailing career from champions such as Dennis Conner, one of the greatest things you can do is surround yourself with a team of experienced (and enthusiastic) people.

In a team sport, the power of the team is all-important—and an experienced team is invaluable when the going gets tough.

• • • • • • • • • • • • IN THEIR OWN WORDS • • • • • • • • • • • •

Buddy Melges

Buddy Melges is a legend in the sport of sailing. With his business (Melges Performance Sailboats) based in Zenda, Wisconsin, the "Wizard of Zenda" is

one of the three helmsmen to have won both an Olympic gold medal (at the
1972 Games in Kiel, Germany) and the America's Cup (in 1992, on board
America³). Buddy is a sailmaker and a boatbuilder by trade and is one of the
most approachable sailors you will find anywhere. Buddy always has the time of
day to help anyone with a question, no matter whether they are a customer of
his or not. His down-to-earth approach to winning sailboats is legendary. I first
met Buddy during my Olympic sailing campaign in the Soling class. By then
he was "the man" in the class and the most loved. I still remember the 1980
Soling Worlds in Ponce, Puerto Rico, when the entire fleet (over fifty boats)
secretly agreed to surprise Buddy by surrounding his boat at the ten-minute gun
before the start of the race and singing "Happy Birthday" to him on his big day.

My first big competition against the world is one I reflect on
quite often.

The event was the 1961 Flying Dutchman (FD) North
American Championship in Chicago on Lake Michigan. I was a
cocky young man of thirty-two, with twenty-six years of sailing
under my belt, and the FD seemed to be the perfect class to test
my skills in international competition. Because my dear friend
Bill Bentsen and I had both been successful in racing Scow class
on Lake Geneva, Wisconsin, we assumed we were ready to compete in the Dutchman. We were wrong at the first gun!

The Chicago race committee set a box course—one mile to
windward, a one-mile beam reach, a one-mile run, and a one-
mile reaching return to the finish. Even though the FD was new
to both of us, we were sure we could go fast on the reaching legs.
Wrong! We were terrible reaching! Luckily, we had only two races
on a box course and managed to finish the regatta in a competitive position. We wanted to compete in the 1964 Olympic Trials
in New Jersey, but we had a lot to learn about the art of reaching.

Time in the boat by ourselves was the only solution, as there
were no fleets nearby. We spent the fall and as much of the winter of
1962 and 1963 as weather permitted sailing alone on Lake Geneva,
followed by a powerboat. We tested speed, sail trim, spinnaker handling, and teamwork. It was rigorous. In March, we competed in FD
Week in St. Petersburg and took second in an eighty-boat fleet.

We ordered a new German FD and were thrilled to win the
U.S. Olympic Trials and to represent our country at the Olympic
Games in Japan, but all was not rosy. The German FDs had a

sheer-height problem that we had to correct before the Games. We performed the surgery suggested by the manufacturer, but now we were at least forty pounds overweight. (After the Olympics, we learned that we'd been the heaviest boat in the fleet.)

But it was tactics, not weight, that cost us the gold medal. I'll focus on two critical races. The third race had winds of 35 knots—a bit overpowering—but we were very fast and were first at the windward mark. We set the chute, just flew for about a quarter mile; then the rudder broke, we broached, and the mast went off the step, severely damaging the deck. In the fourth race, we led to the finish line, but misread the favored end and finished second. We were honored to receive a bronze medal.

Lesson learned? Clearly, the time we spent practicing and perfecting our skills in the Flying Dutchman helped these two inland lake sailors achieve world-class speed. Critical, too, was Bill's ability with the finer points of boat trim, tuning, technique, equipment, and the racing rules.

Attitude was key. Looking back, I have to admit that we were quite awed by winning the 1964 U.S. Olympic Trials and competing at an Olympics. It's hard not to be. But awe affects focus. By the 1970s, when we started our preparations to campaign a Soling—with Scow sailor Bill Allan as the third crew—we set our sights on winning the 1972 Olympics at Kiel, Germany, not just getting there. The Trials on San Francisco Bay were a challenge, but we were no longer wide-eyed. We were a team, and we'd done our homework. This time we'd looked beyond the Trials. We knew our stuff was fast—sails, rig, crew, everything—and we were totally confident. We smoked 'em.

* *

Leadership: Different Strokes

There isn't just one right way to lead a team or one right way to succeed. Individuality is a huge factor in sports and competition. Having sailed with skippers as diverse in their backgrounds and personal styles of leadership as Ted Turner, Dennis Conner, Russell Coutts, George David, and Roy Disney, I've noticed that there are as many different styles of leadership as there are leaders.

And while there are certain things that all good leaders do, an effective leadership style has to fit the person. You can't fake good leadership. In the same way, the "culture" of the team has to fit the individuals for them to be successful.

Consider the culture of Emirates Team New Zealand during the course of the 32nd America's Cup held off the coast of Valencia in 2007. The team was famous for never showing emotion—no high-fives, no hand-shaking, no smiles or pats on the back. Nothing. When the team won a race (and they won plenty), the win was duly noted by the sailors—without emotion—but then it was on to the next step.

For those of us watching the team from the outside, this approach was almost maddening—it seemed almost inhuman. Were these guys all being brainwashed by their leader, famed ocean racer Grant Dalton?

The next summer I sailed in a race with Ray Davies, strategist for that 2007 New Zealand team that won the Louis Vuitton Cup Trials before being beaten by *Alinghi* in the Cup Finals. We were racing together in the Rolex Maxi Worlds in Sardinia aboard an American boat. Ray was the tactician and I was serving as his strategist. Every race of the four-race series was a tight battle between our boat, *Rambler*, and the newer and faster *Alfa Romeo*, from Australia. All tied up after two races, we sailed a great third race, and according to our timekeeping, we had won handicap honors by seconds. We double-checked our stopwatches, and then, as soon as we returned to shore, sent a crew member to the scoreboard to see if we'd won. He returned all smiles, and our twenty-four-man crew knew immediately—we had won!

Caught up in the emotion of the moment, I turned to Ray and raised my open hand above my head—offering the international symbol for a high five. He reacted without thinking and naturally raised up his hand, smiled, and slapped my hand with a resounding *whack*. A minute later he turned to me and begged privately—out of earshot of the crew— "Don't ever do that to me again!"

The next day, in a team meeting on the boat, he said, "One of the things I noticed during yesterday's race is that there was some emotion being shown on the boat. We've really got to work hard just being very steady and keep sailing the same way all the time—no matter whether we're doing well or poorly."

Ray Davies was brought up in this particular culture, and he believes in it. It's the way he leads, and his team is in sync with him. We ended up winning that World Championship aboard *Rambler*, and Ray's contribution was immense.

But another successful skipper I know has a completely different leadership style, and it works for him and his team. Vasco Vascotto is a very successful and flamboyant Italian sailor. He's well known for his success on the race course and his leadership of big-boat teams. He's always outspoken. He's always smiling and just a great, fun character in the sport—a breath of fresh air.

In an interview during an America's Cup exhibition series where he was sailing with an all-Italian team, he said, "One of the things that's so important for me, and what I like about this all-Italian team, is we can all do what we want to do—and that's to show our emotion. When we win, we're very, very happy. And when we lose, we're very, very sad."

Here are two great sailors and team leaders—both very successful, and both espousing completely different philosophies regarding the show of emotion within the team. It just goes to prove there isn't any one right way to lead. A leader's style has to fit the team—it has to fit the people. They have to believe in him and have an investment in the team's culture if they hope to have any chance for success in the long run.

At the same time, a team is made up of individual people—each with his or her own goals and motivations. To get the most out of each member of the team, leaders need to understand *all* of their people—they need to know what motivates them and what makes them tick. Different people respond differently to any variety of leadership approaches. By knowing each member of your team, you can deliver the right input at the right time—maximizing the performance of individual team members, and raising the performance level of your entire team.

Preparing to Race

In *any* competitive environment, the only way you're going to be successful is if you are well prepared—you're mentally ready, you have a good team, you've practiced, you have good equipment, and you're ready for racing. But guess what? *Everybody* comes to a big event prepared. The goal of preparation—and of practice—is to make yourself one step better than the competition.

So *my* focus when I prepare for a race is not my competition, it's *me*.

The only thing you can really control in a race (or in life, for that matter) is yourself, and to some extent your team, your boat, and your boat's equipment. To somehow try to be better than someone else doesn't really focus you on the real task at hand, which is improving your *own* sailing and improving your *own* performance.

I have found that it pays to constantly assess the strengths and weaknesses of me and my team, and then to work up a realistic process for building on the strengths while focusing on the weaknesses. By working on the overall process, you'll end up improving your level.

Part of the improvement can be found through well-structured practice, and by getting better equipment, getting better crew, and getting more fit. But that's only part of the equation of being truly prepared to compete.

You become prepared to compete by competing.

I'm a firm believer that practice—while important—is not enough. For me, an important element in improving my own performance is to actually get out there and compete.

Look at Lance Armstrong. He retired from bicycle racing after winning an unprecedented seven Tour de France titles. He then decided to leave retirement behind and mount a challenge for the 2010 Tour de France. For him this didn't mean just spinning in the gym or training with teammates. It meant laying it on the line in actual road races—getting beaten up by the young bucks as he built up his condition to be ready for the Tour. Here's a guy who's used to winning, but he lost his first two races after hitting the comeback trail. And he didn't lose by just a few seconds or even minutes. He finished twenty-third in his first race and seventh in his second. Lance knows that real race preparation in his sport means mixing actual competition with physical training. There's no practice session in the world that can simulate the tactical and mental challenge of a real race. Sailing is the same.

Sure, you can practice certain aspects of sailboat racing— you can practice your tacks or jibes and cut valuable seconds off your time on the race course. Or you can work with sail designers to tweak your sail shapes that will make your boat a tenth of a knot faster in a particular wind condition. But ultimately you have to apply your whole package in a real-life situation—in battle—where the playing field can be quite a bit different than in practice.

I've learned a lot about the benefits of race practice from one-design guru and former Star world champion Vince Brun. He taught me that the classic two- or three-boat speed-testing format—where boats line up side by side and drag-race for miles to find out which sail or setting is fastest—is flawed. This is because lots of things happen on the race course that don't occur regularly in a practice situation—even if you have one or two other good boats to practice against. Vince believes that you're forced to sail your boat differently in a race than in a controlled practice situation—and he's right. An important difference in a race is that you are forced to change gears—that is, to change sailing modes quickly not just because of the wind and wave conditions, but by the proximity of your competitors.

Coming off the starting line close-hauled in a fleet race, for example, you usually can't go as fast as you would in open water. At a start you're usually surrounded by boats that constrain your sailing style. You often have to sail in a different "gear" just to keep your wind clear and get your boat positioned into a clean lane. This may mean "pinching" for a minute or two—or maybe easing sails and reaching off to get clear of your neighbors on the starting line. Once you work your way into open water you can turn on the afterburners and let it rip. The sooner you can, the better.

Now that's fleet racing—where I strongly believe that race practice should be part of any team's preparation. But because the America's Cup is a match race, if your team has a good enough trial horse boat and crew, you can actually replicate real competition in house. But even so, it's like Michael Jordan just playing against Magic Johnson all the time. While it's not a bad way to practice, you might become a better all-around basketball player if you took on some different competitors from time to time—say, a Kobe Bryant or a LeBron James.

The ultimate goal in a race is to be the best you can be, and all these elements of practice and preparation help get you there. If at the end of the day you leave nothing on the table, that's all anybody can ask. And if somebody beats you, well, that's sport. If you could win *all* the time, it'd be too easy and the sense of accomplishment might be diminished.

How to Read the Wind

One of the first things a new sailor learns is that the entire sailing universe revolves around the wind. The direction from which the wind blows—and its strength—dictate where the boat can sail, how fast you can go in a certain direction, what sails you can put up, and whether you can even go sailing at all.

On the race course, being able to react to changes in the wind makes the difference between winning and losing.

And change the wind does. The wind is always increasing, decreasing, and changing in one place compared to another. Whether you're sailing a short 10 minute leg up to a buoy or thousands of miles across the ocean, understanding the wind and being able to predict (or at least have an educated guess about) what it's going to do from minute to minute will give you an edge on the competition.

But this is a difficult proposition. It's not like a pro golfer looking at the putting green with his caddie and figuring out that it's sloping to the left here and a little to the right here—and then he goes and knocks off a 50-foot putt that goes right, then left, then into the hole.

Rarely is life that straightforward in sailing.

Unlike a putting green, the wind is constantly changing. If the wind was stronger on one side the last time you sailed a particular course, that doesn't necessarily mean it's going to be stronger on that side the next time. So being able to use your eyes to see the wind is a fundamental skill that must be honed for all sailors, especially when racing on a short course. But what exactly are you looking for?

Four-time Olympic medalist Valentin Mankin from Russia had a great quote that we discovered and loved to repeat when we sailed in college. He said that he sees wind "like colors on the water."

In fact you do look for the "colors" of the wind on the open water—the lighter shades caused by fewer ripples in areas of less wind and the darker shades caused by more ripples that are indicative of more breeze. You must train your eyes to look for these subtle but all-important differences in color that provide a road map for the racer. I remember the first time I sailed with Terry Hutchinson, the multitalented professional sailor from Annapolis who has had so much success in recent years in so many different classes—from Melges 24s to Farr 40s to the America's Cup. He was fresh out of college, and my longtime match racing teammate, Moose McClintock, brought him along to sail with us in the Knickerbocker Cup Match Race in Long Island Sound. The first thing that struck me was how focused and talented he was at seeing the wind on the water. We soon were comfortable relying on his calls, which were spot on. To put it simply, the goal is to pick a course where you sail the maximum amount of time in the darker (windier) patches of water and avoid the lighter-looking (less wind) regions like the plague.

There are other visual cues to see wind strength and direction, too. If you are lucky, you can key off of other sailboats. Their angle of heel is often the best tip-off of wind speed, and their heading is an indicator of wind direction. Racing boats are better references than day sailors and cruisers because you can better rely that they are being sailed well—at a true upwind or downwind angle and not spearing off on some random reaching course with the possible aid of an engine. Look for any external cue that can give you an edge on predicting the wind. Sometimes there are flags or smokestacks on shore that can tell you a lot. But most of the time, it's just the open water from which you must glean your information. Remember, what you're looking for is color or shading differences between areas where there are fewer ripples on the water and more ripples on the water.

Practice makes perfect, so constantly look for ways to practice your wind-finding skills. For example, if you take off in an airplane over the water and look down, you'll see that some places look glassy while some have little ripples on them. Ripples created by a puff of wind will appear darker on the water. So that's what we are looking for—darker water!

I'm amazed at how many new sailors don't just open their eyes more—there's nothing that I'm doing that you couldn't do yourself. It's not years of practice that tell me to go to the right side to get more wind. Before the start of a race I'll often stand in my boat (the higher your vantage point the easier it is to see the wind on the water) and look to try to pick the place where there's the most wind speed. But only rarely can you tell the exact direction from which the wind is blowing by looking at the water. Maybe you can get it within five or ten degrees, but seldom can you see wind on the water and say, "Oh, that's a right-hand shift [or a left-hand shift]."

There are cases in lake sailing where stronger wind, from higher up in the atmosphere, will sink down to the surface making a distinctive shape on the water called a "cat's paw." It will appear on the water as a dark arc shape, and the wind will fan outward from that initial puff. The wind direction will usually fan out, too. So if you are sailing upwind on the left edge of the cat's paw, you experience a right-hand shift compared to a boat that is on the right edge.

There are times when you can notice a consistent trend of wind shift by watching the clouds and their position relative to you. For that reason it always pays to watch the sky as well as the water's surface and try to build a wind shift theory based on the clouds. But don't get lost looking at the sky, because the water's surface is usually where the best telltale signs are available. It's all about looking for the stronger wind (darker water) and sailing in the longer puffs while trying to stay away from the glassy patches. Sometimes, on a really shifty, puffy day, we call this type of sailing "connecting the dots."

Because the wind is so changeable, you really want to focus on what the wind on the course looks like in the last few minutes before the starting gun. At about three minutes before the gun, try to build in some time to have a conversation with the crew and discuss what they see. A lot of times among the afterguard of a boat, that's the type of conversation that's going on: "What do you think?" "Do you like the right?" "Where is there a better breeze now?" When reading the wind, it definitely pays to keep an open mind and open eyes.

• • • • • • • • • • • RACER'S RULES • • • • • • • • • • •
Tom Whidden

Tom Whidden, CEO of North Sails, is one of the most experienced America's Cup sailors in the world. He sailed with Dennis Conner in seven America's Cup campaigns, beginning in 1979. He was tactician in six America's Cup series, winning three times. Tom and I go way back, and there is no one I enjoy racing with more. His sense of humor is second to none, and his tactical skills are uncanny—Tom rarely makes a bad call. Here are some of Tom's racing rules:

1. The most precious commodity is time.
2. Balance risk and reward.
3. Push accountability as far down the ranks as possible.
4. Have a game plan.
5. If it ain't broke, fix it anyway.
6. Don't be afraid to make decisions.
7. Keep on an even keel emotionally.
8. Never let up!
9. Show them it's not bad to make a decision and be wrong.
10. If you act like a winner, it's easy to win.
11. If you don't have a competitive edge, don't compete.

• •

Feel the Heel

"That's it—feel the heel—don't worry about the instruments or telltales so much, just keep this angle of heel steady."

How many times have I said something like this when coaching helmsmen in keelboats? One of the biggest mistakes I see helmsmen make when sailing is letting the wind push their boat around.

Years ago I attended a seminar where Olympic gold medalist and America's Cup winner Buddy Melges was on the panel. He said he can be sitting on his porch looking at a group of boats sailing along on a breezy, puffy day on Lake Geneva (his home lake in Wisconsin) and tell which one is fastest just by its angle of heel. "The boat that keeps a more consistent angle of heel through all the puffs and lulls will be fastest," said Buddy. To help create the consistency that he's looking for, Melges said that one of the key things he watches when he's steering is the angle the headstay makes with the horizon.

The goal on a keelboat is to find that sweet angle of heel and keep it there. In fact, yacht designers have computer programs that can predict not only the target boat speed for any angle of sail and wind speed, but also the target heel angle where the boat will be fastest. I've been on larger keelboats where the "heel target" (target boat speed for the current heel angle) is a valuable reference for the trimmer and helmsman when sailing upwind. It's especially helpful on days (common in the spring when the water is cold) when there's lots of wind shear or a funky gradient where the wind speed at the top of the mast is much different from the wind speed in the middle of the sail plan. But this chapter is not about the instruments, it's about using your senses to feel the heel and steer and trim the boat to keep the heel angle consistent.

The goal changes on most centerboard boats (dinghies) because they sail fastest when sailed with no or very little heel. So on a puffy day in a dinghy, you have to sail the boat using a lot of kinetics when sailing upwind. Olympic coach Skip Whyte had a mantra for those days when the puffs were coming like stings on the water: "Ease, hike, trim." The end result is that the boat doesn't heel when the puff hits—it moves forward. Just like on a keelboat, the helmsman has to be super sensitive to the angle of heel—even on a dinghy.

On a keelboat in puffy conditions, your extra hiking may not be so effective and you can play the sails, but usually not as quickly as on a dinghy. But you can steer—carefully and with finesse—to maintain a steady angle of heel until the sails can be readjusted. On a bigger keelboat, it really helps to have a crew calling the wind to help the helmsman anticipate the puffs and the lulls. Here's an example of good communication: "Steady wind for the next fifteen seconds, then a slow build coming. . . . Moderate puff in five seconds—this one will last for fifteen seconds."

The bottom line is that the driver needs to be acutely aware of the boat's angle of heel and how his steering can affect that heel. In many conditions, the speedometer and the telltales on the luff of the jib (or the curl of the spinnaker when sailing downwind) are less important inputs than just feeling the heel. Buddy's advice is worth its weight in gold— the boat that controls its angle of heel best will usually be the fastest.

Motivation: Getting 110 Percent from Your Team

Some people just seem to have a natural talent for getting the very best out of those with whom they work (or race). Some do it through charisma or the sheer force of their personalities. Others do it by setting a good example—walking their talk. Yet others do it by using carrots and sticks. Ted Turner—founder of Turner Broadcasting and former vice chairman of Time Warner, Inc.—has his own approach: use every trick in the book.

I'll never forget the time we were sailing together in the Admiral's Cup regatta off the coast of southern England. Back then, the Admiral's Cup was "the" ocean racing event, a battle among national teams—three boats per country. We were representing the United States. It was the middle of the second night of the Channel Race, and Ted was at the helm of our 43-foot boat *Locura*, owned by George de Guardiola and Ricardo Vadia, a pair of developers from South Florida who became my good griends. Along with Ted, four or five of us were on deck, standing our watch. We were all sleep-deprived; it was dark, cold, and wet (classic English Channel conditions); and the breeze was dying.

Suddenly we spotted the white stern light of one of the competitors twinkling off in the distance, maybe half a mile ahead of us. It was one of the Italian boats. They were in the lead, and we were catching up to them. In the pitch dark it was not clear how we were making our gains—maybe it's because we were a little bit closer to shore than the Italians, giving us a little bit more breeze, or maybe it was just that the Italians were sleepier than we were. Whatever the reason, *Locura* was hooked up and starting to move faster and faster.

As we gradually closed in on the Italians, Ted got more excited with each passing minute. He began a constant stream of talk to the crew—exhorting every man on deck to concentrate on trimming the sails to take advantage of the slightest puff of wind and to move their weight to keep the angle of heel steady. The closer we got to the Italian boat, the more excited Ted got—I'll bet they could hear us!

We were already plenty motivated. We all wanted to win, to come from behind and beat the Italians. As we were all working hard to catch up, Ted went all-in: "Come on, you guys—work hard here. Concentrate—we're catching them. Ease that spinnaker six inches. If we pass these guys, I'll give everyone on deck ten thousand dollars! Come on—work hard!"

It took us an hour of intense concentration, but we ended up catching and then passing the Italians. Did we really care about the ten-thousand-dollar offer? Probably not; it came completely from left field amidst Ted's escalating exhortations. For those of us on the crew, winning was all that mattered at that moment. We were already motivated. But you know what? During that hour that Ted was driving—maintaining a running monologue throughout—none of us thought of how tired we were. We totally forgot about how cold our feet were in the sea boots. As we gained on the Italians, Ted knew exactly how to take us to an even higher level of performance. And each of us gave everything he had—and maybe a little more. To this day, I can still feel the buzz of the intensity on deck that night.

And I never even thought of asking Ted for my share! He seems to have a pretty good feel of where his money can best be used these days.

When the Going Gets Rough

Racing in extreme conditions, when the wind is screaming and the waves have the force to really knock your boat around, takes a lot of experience coupled with a very safety-conscious approach toward running the boat. Even in the heat of an important race, the best sailors will, at times, slow the boat down to avoid breakdowns or catastrophe. A common storm situation where things can get extra nasty is when the waves are coming from a direction other than from where the wind is blowing. If the "old" wind was, say, coming from the south, and there's been a wind shift and the wind is now coming from the west, then if your course is southbound, you'll be sailing on a fast and powerful point of sail—a beam reach with a 90-degree wind angle— but the waves will be coming straight at you. Get some current going against those waves, and those launch ramps will start to stack up and get really steep. Before you know it, you can get into a situation where the boat or the mast simply will not survive the pounding when sailing at 100 percent, full-speed.

My college roommate, Stan Honey, is one of the most respected navigators in the world, and lately he's been sailing a lot of maxi catamarans in ocean races and record attempts.

He tells me that part of the tactics of routing these boats is to find the smoother water, because as soon as the seas get rough, you have to rein them in and slow down. For example, in a recent west-to-east transatlantic record attempt, he learned that it was better to forgo the 3-knot boost from the eastbound Gulf Stream current. It was so rough in the Stream that the boat speed had to be dropped back by more than the advantage of the speed boost from the current. His big trimaran made better time by changing course and dropping out of the Gulf Stream where the seas were much smoother.

Knowing when to ease off on the speed is critically important, and it's something that every good sailor learns when racing in extreme conditions. Another essential consideration in rough weather is making sure the crew is safe and secure. Before every overnight race and anytime the conditions are expected to get rough, it's important to have a full-crew meeting to review the boat's man-overboard procedure and the roles each of us will each play if someone goes over. At this meeting the crew should be apprised of the location of all safety gear, including life jackets, safety harnesses, flashlights, EPIRB(s), and ditch bags, and should discuss abandon-ship procedures. This is also a good time to talk about the boat's rules with respect to wearing life harnesses. Although wearing a life jacket or safety harness is always an individual choice, the watch captain or the person in charge on deck can always make the call for the crew to don their harnesses when the going gets rough. In rough weather, they're used all the time. Wearing the harness is one step (and a lot of the modern harnesses have a built-in inflatable life jacket) toward crew safety, but it'll do you no good if the tether is not clipped to a secure point. When the going gets extreme, everybody looks out for everybody else.

I'll be the first to admit that it's a pain in the neck to wear life harnesses. They're cumbersome. They're a pain to put on. They're difficult to find at night when you wake up and you're going on deck. But they can save your life if you're clipped in and a wave sends you over the side of the boat—that is, until your tether takes up and you find that you're still—miraculously—on deck.

In extreme conditions, you've got to move carefully—especially down below. When you're on deck, it's easier to get around because you're already pretty aware of the motion of the boat and the oncoming waves, so you can pause for a moment until the boat steadies out before moving to the next handhold, or you can hang on while the boat dives into a wave and throws green water across the entire deck. But down below you don't see the seas coming—it's a random roller-coaster ride! And on some boats there are some pretty big wide-open areas down below that don't have any handholds. Some of the worst sailing accidents I've seen and heard about occur down below, where a crew is getting ready to put on some clothes or walking from one area to the other on the boat and the boat moves unexpectedly and they fall. In extreme conditions, moving slowly and carefully often means doing so on your hands and knees, even down below deck.

One of my first overnight races taught me a lesson I'll never forget. It was a cold and windy spring night, and we were sailing upwind in the 45-foot sloop *Dynamite.* The coffeepot was whistling down below, and the owner went to mix up a brew. As he was grabbing the pot, the boat lurched and boiling water went all over his legs. We immediately dropped out and headed to shore to get him treatment. Lesson learned. *Always* wear your foul weather pants when working with boiling water in the galley anytime there is the possibility of unexpected motion.

Communication

My friend Chuck Robinson, former Nike board member and U.S. deputy secretary of state, has a slightly racy maxim that he loves to share whenever he can: "Communication is the essence of success—in the boardroom and in the bedroom."

I have personally found that Chuck's axiom, stressing the importance of communication, applies in just about all aspects of life. And this one really resonates with me.

Although I grew up sailing dinghies, the majority of my racing in recent years has been on much larger boats, where communication gets increasingly difficult because of the sheer size of the crew and the background noise on board. To address this problem, which is exacerbated by helicopter noise during the televised races, America's Cup teams routinely use custom-built electronic communication devices. These fancy units often employ in-ear technology that is lightweight but waterproof to allow the sailors to get the message back and forth in the cock-pit, up to the foredeck—and even up atop the mast, where a crew member is often hoisted in light winds to get a better perspective on the winds. Typically only a few members of the crew are issued these units, and some devices may only be able to receive and not transmit to keep the chatter to a minimum. Usually these include one or two members of the afterguard, the sail trimmer, the pitman, and the bowman.

When I'm in charge of organizing a team on a bigger boat, we rarely have access to this esoteric communications gear. However, I use the same sort of communications stream-lining by selecting only a few members of the team I will be talking to during a race. Using this relatively small communi-cation chain on the boat, I then count on the members of that chain to convey the message farther around the boat as needed without the distraction of lots of yelling. Before our first day of practice, we'll discuss this simplified communication network with the entire crew so that everybody knows how the information will flow.

The saying "a quiet boat is a happy boat" is true—having twenty people expressing their opinions simultaneously during a key moment in the race is not good for organization. Even so, Chuck Robinson's adage still applies. So when I, as tactician standing in the back of the boat, want to communicate something about boat speed or performance, I'll direct my comments to the mainsail trimmer. Since I'm usually standing behind the helmsman, I know that he hears the message too, and I'll count on the headsail trimmer getting the message, if necessary, from the mainsail trimmer.

If there is an upcoming maneuver requiring a headsail change (such as a spinnaker set when rounding a mark), the entire crew needs to be on the same page and in the loop. But on a big 70-footer with more than twenty crew, I'll convey my thoughts and plans directly just to the pitman. He is my communication node positioned forward in the boat, halfway between the helmsman and the bow. Not only does he need to know the plan so he can organize the hoisting and lowering of the sails, but he's also perfectly positioned to pass on the plan to the foredeck team. I figure that everyone in the cockpit behind the pitman will probably hear my plans, too.

The key to using this node system of communication is that everyone on the boat knows it's being used, and they know who the closest node is to them in case they have questions. Even though the nodes are in place, I want the crew to keep their eyes open, and I use an open-door policy in the back of the boat, where anyone can yell to me to provide some information I may not see. The crew then uses their best judgment so they don't overload me with obvious information or interrupt me during a critical moment.

Sometimes—especially during the prestart maneuvering —the tactician must bypass the pitman node and communicate directly to the bowman, who can be out of voice range when the ropes are screaming on the winches during a maneuver. A lot of this communication can be most effectively done using hand signals, something that is set up before the start of the race.

But even with a practiced crew with an established communications hierarchy, things can go wrong. An example is when I was sailing aboard *Titan*, a 75-foot sloop, during Antigua Sailing Week. We were coming up to a mark on a spinnaker run, and the next leg looked like it would require a jibe maneuver, sailing on a tight spinnaker reach for about a mile and then dropping the spinnaker and hoisting the jib.

The pitman happened to be in the back of the boat for a moment (making a "pit stop," so to speak), so I reviewed with him my current thinking, which was different than what we'd discussed in our prerace meeting. I told him that the wind angle on the next leg would allow us to carry the spinnaker for about a quarter of the leg before having to change to a jib. Because I made this decision privately in the back of the boat, only the pitman and members of the afterguard were aware of the change of plan.

As we rounded the mark, I instructed the helmsman to turn up onto the new course and get the boat ripping quickly. At that very moment, however, the crew in the forward part of the boat began the spinnaker takedown maneuver. I quickly realized that the two halves of the boat (front and back) were on diametrically opposed pages, but it was too late. The spinnaker fell into the water and soon all of us were up on the foredeck trying to drag the spinnaker (which had been dropped straight into the water) back on deck. Meanwhile, the boat was sailing at about half speed and our competitors were gaining—all precipitated by a communication breakdown.

Lesson learned . . . again. Communication is the essence of success, in the boardroom and on the race course.

～～～

Sail Trim Fundamentals

Sure—sail trim is important to racers. Small adjustments to the controls that shape the sail can make the difference between being able to hang in a tight spot during a race and being shot out the back. But just like many things in life, until you have the basics covered, tweaking the little details is really just spinning wheels. So let's talk about the basic priorities of sail trim.

During college, my summertime job was teaching sailing to kids (not that much younger than I was) at the Noroton Yacht Club junior sailing program on western Long Island Sound in Connecticut. I learned many lessons during those three years teaching summer sailing, but one didn't come to roost until about ten years later, when my students started reappearing on boats and in my life as my peers. When you are nineteen, a fifteen-year-old seems a lot younger than you. But a few more laps around the sun, and that difference seems immaterial. So I'm glad I treated those "kids" with friendship and respect back then, because some of them are still good friends (and even clients) today.

But we're talking about the lesson I learned back then about sail trim—about how important following some simple basics of setting up your sails will get you to the 98th percentile of performance. Since Noroton YC had a strong tradition in racing, the sailing program was structured to help the kids learn to race. In the beginning of the season, after watching a few days of sailing, I decided that it was not yet time to teach the kids about the intricacies of sail trim—they first needed to learn and become consistent with the sail trim basics.

That holds true in any harbor in the world, where with rare exceptions every sailboat I see needs a lesson in those same basics. So rather than diving into the aerodynamic principles of lift and how different foil shapes are appropriate for different conditions, here are the basics—what I taught my kids about sail trim many years ago. Most of these principles apply in light and moderate winds.

Get it up.   There's almost always more wind higher up in the atmosphere, so get your sails up in the breeze! Mainsails and jibs should be hoisted to their proper tension. When trimmed and sailing upwind in light and moderate winds, the sail should have a few wrinkles at the lower front edge (luff) of the sail that would be erased with another half an inch of hoist (or downward cunningham tension). The best way to get to this sweet spot is to hoist the sail a little too much and then trim in the sheet and fill the sail—often the halyard will stretch and the tension will be correct. If not, then ease the halyard until loose wrinkles *just* begin to appear in the luff of the sail. In strong winds, the halyard should be tensioned a bit more (at least one inch on a 20-foot boat) until all those luff wrinkles just disappear. The windier it is, the tighter the luff should be tensioned with the halyard (or cunningham if the halyard is at max hoist). At the dock, or when the sail is not trimmed in, the luff tension will appear to be much too tight.

Going upwind, steer to the sails.   When sailing upwind, the main and jib sheets should be pulled in almost as tight as they can be pulled, and then the driver should steer a course to that sail trim. Telltales (yarns) attached near the leading edge (luff) of the jib show the direction of the airflow and are invaluable early indicators of a "stalled" sail. These telltales are also incredibly helpful to the helmsman to stay in the upwind groove.

Trim to the course on a reach.   When sailing on a reach, do the opposite. Steer a straight (desired) course and adjust the sheet tensions of the sails to keep them correctly trimmed in the groove. The general rule of sail trim applies: When in doubt, let it out. Sails have this great way of telling you when they are undertrimmed—they flap like flags. But a sail that is over-trimmed doesn't have such an obvious indicator—it looks just like a perfectly trimmed sail. Since the maximum power from a sail is achieved when the sail is trimmed to the edge of luff-ing—just tight enough to eliminate all but the smallest signs of luffing along the leading edge—it makes sense that you should always be easing the sail to test it and see if it begins to luff along its leading edge. If it does, you had the sheet tension set correct. If it doesn't luff, well, it's a good thing you eased it, because it was overtrimmed, and you should keep easing until you see that small bubble of a luff indicating that you are right on that per-fect angle of attack for your sail foil.

Block the flow on a run.   When sailing on a run, the sails are no longer working like an airfoil, they are simply a barn door catching the wind, so set the mainsail so the boom is perpendicular to the wind direction. The jib doesn't do much on a run, so put up your spinnaker if you have one.

Once you have the basics of sail hoist and sheet tension sorted out, you will be looking pretty good and getting most of the power out of your sails. Your next step in sail trim hier-archy will be to get the tension of the back edge of the sail (leech tension) set correctly. Upwind leech tension on the mainsail is controlled with the mainsheet. You can get in the ballpark by sighting up from under the middle of the boom and looking at the angle of the topmost batten. If it's a long batten, look at the angle of its back 20 percent relative to the angle of the boom, which is probably on centerline unless it's quite windy. The back (aft) edge of the upper leech (at the height of the top batten) should be parallel to the boom. If the mainsheet is too tight, the leech of the mainsail will be closed and the batten will not be parallel to the boom; its back edge will be pointed out to windward. If the mainsheet is too loose, the batten will not be parallel to the boom, either, but the back edge of the upper leech will be pointed off to leeward.

Off the wind on a reach and run, the mainsail's leech tension (or twist) is controlled by the boom vang. The basic rule of thumb is to pull the vang until it is just taut when sailing upwind with proper trim, then ease it a couple of inches and cleat it.

Getting the jib's leech tension correct is a bit different. Like the mainsail, the sheet tension controls the sail's angle of attack to the wind, but it also affects leech tension. The position of the jib lead (the pulley or fairlead through which the jib sheet runs on its way from the clew of the jib to the winch or cleat) affects leech tension, too. Usually the lead can be adjusted forward or back along some sort of a track. Get the lead position wrong and the jib trim can look awful. A good general rule is to sail upwind with the jib sheet taut and observe the angle of the jib sheet as it comes from the lead to the sail. It should equally bisect the angle of the corner of the sail. That is, if you drew an extension of the imaginary path of the jib sheet onto the sail, it would split that corner of the jib (the clew) into two equal angles. Err on the side of having the lead too far forward rather than too far aft.

Despite all these fine-tuning controls, remember that a sail's sheet is the most important sail trim control, and the Golden Rule of sail trim always applies: When in doubt, let it out (a little).

Why I Sail

I'm often asked why I sail and why I race.

Of course, my professional career has revolved around sailing, so an easy answer is that "it's my job." But the good news is that my real answer to this question has not varied since I first felt the wind press into a sail and the splash of the spray coming off the bow: I love sailing and everything about it, and I can't get enough of it.

I was a baseball player and, gasp, a power boater until I was thirteen years old, when my family moved from Cincinnati, Ohio, to Rowayton, Connecticut, on Long Island Sound. Granted, I have always loved being on and around the water, but that never would have led me into sailboat racing except that across the street from our new Connecticut home, as luck would have it, was a family of sailors. The kids (BJ, Doug, and Bill) were all close to my age and their parents were into sailing big time. The father, Ted Jones, who at the time was an editor of what is now *Sailing World* magazine, arranged for the local yacht club to bend the rules so that my brother and I (non-members) could attend the summer junior sailing program.

Even though I was starting about three years later than most of my peers, I loved sailing from the get-go. Still, my first time out single-handing a Dyer Dhow was far from propitious: I got the boat stuck in irons—dead in the water—and the instructor finally came up to me in a motorboat and observed cynically, "You don't know how to sail, do you." He was absolutely right, and I felt about one inch tall. But it wasn't long before I knew my leech from my luff and was immersing myself in the Jones family maritime library in the winter months when I couldn't be sailing. In the next few years I spent a lot of time crewing aboard a Lightning—the classic 19-foot one-design sloop I still remember very fondly. It wasn't until just before college that I started putting time on the helm. I loved the water and I loved being out on it. It's partly communing with nature; it's partly being out in the great outdoors; it's partly "the call of the sea"—all of those things, and more.

Sailing is a pretty remarkable thing. It's a magical harnessing of the wind's power to make a boat move. But I guess you'd have to characterize me as a pretty competitive personality. I have a force driving me when I'm out on the water—I always want to be sailing fast. If in a race, I want to do well, and I have very high expectations. I feel that through my experience and all the time I've devoted to the sport, I can make a huge difference on any boat, and I'm very proud when I do. I've passed the point where I'm worried about what people think of me on the boat, and in my line of work I set foot into a lot of different situations with a lot of different personalities. But I'm confident and comfortable enough in my broad background in the sport that I can slot into just about any position on any team and make a difference. If I'm the team leader, great. If somebody else is in charge, well, I'll do my best to play my part and try to learn from him.

Although at times in my career I've been totally focused on something extremely complex and encompassing—such as an America's Cup campaign—I also really enjoy getting back to my roots and sailing in a simple small boat and doing a weekend local race, or getting out on a sailboard and just shredding along. Because sailing has so many different facets, you can continue to learn throughout your life. I think *that* more than anything has kept me going in the sport, because I still have plenty to learn.

The art of sailing still turns me on. I love making a sailboat go fast.

~~~

Commitment to the Commitment

If I added up all the time I've spent sailing with Dennis Conner over the past three decades—as a part of his *Stars & Stripes* America's Cup teams, and in countless races in San Diego and around the world—I'll bet the total would be in *years*, not just days or weeks or even months. DC is the consummate racing sailor. He is "Mr. America's Cup," having won it four times. His record of national and world sailing titles in an incredible variety of boats is amazing. Even today, years after his America's Cup victories, when he enters a race, the media take notice, and the competition starts to sweat.

I've learned a lot from Dennis, but I think one of the most important lessons he's taught me has to do with the power of commitment.

Partway through the historic 1987 *Stars & Stripes* America's Cup campaign, Dennis called a rare meeting with the entire team one evening after dinner. We were all tired from a long and hard day of sailing, but we knew that something special was going on—something we wouldn't want to miss. In the entire history of the campaign, Dennis had never called all one hundred of us together for a meeting.

What we got that evening was the distillation of DC's personal philosophy of competition—and a glimpse deep into the heart of a champion.

DC got up after our meal and started his talk. He explained how everyone has their own level to which they normally perform, and over the course of the campaign we had all unknowingly raised our own comfort level day by day. By training hard—for months on end, in the strong winds and huge ocean waves off the southern coast of

Oahu—we had learned to feel *comfortable* sailing a 50,000-pound, 12 Meter sloop in 25 knots of wind. Despite losing men overboard, the sail blowouts, the broken gear, and even the bruised and battered bodies, each of us had made real personal progress—raising our comfort level of performance. Dennis pointed out that each of us, by making our "commitment to the commitment," had worked harder as a group—and together we had raised our own game to the point where we were on the verge of winning the America's Cup. That was not a position anyone—no matter *how* talented—could just walk into.

Dennis was right. A year before, we were all gifted individuals, newly formed into a professional team. But none of us would have been comfortable being in the position we were in now—closing in on a historic victory. By committing to make a commitment to win—and by committing to one another, to our teammates—we raised our own standards to a much higher level. Because of this commitment, our team had developed along with our boat. And I honestly believe that there is no team on earth that could have stopped us from winning the Cup back for the United States. We were, in the truest sense of the term, *unstoppable*. The Australian defenders aboard *Kookaburra* soon discovered this as we swept them 4–0 and took the Cup back home to the United States.

Big Joe's Top Five Sailing Mistakes

When I was racing in college, our archrival in the New England district was the team from Tufts University, coached by the legendary and charismatic Joe Duplin. Joe was a no-nonsense Star class world champion from Boston, and he approached the sport of sailing very matter-of-factly. Although the varsity racing team was his main focus, part of Joe's job was running the sailing club, which offered learn-to-sail lessons to undergraduates. Joe was not big on intro-ductory classroom lessons. Instead, he'd pop a new wannabe freshman sailor into a dinghy on the dock at Tufts's Mystic Lake boathouse, hand the student the mainsheet, and say, "Here's your accelerator. You pull this in, and the boat speeds up. You want to slow down, you let it out." Then he'd hand over the hiking stick and say, "This is your steering wheel. When you want to turn left, pull it to the right. When you want to turn right, push it to the left." With those simple pearls of Duplin wisdom still ringing in the air, he would give the boat a big push and send the new sailor out . . . to sink or swim!

Although Joe was legendary in his pursuit of a boat speed edge through technology tweaks, weight reduction, and boat preparation, in college sailing all the boats are the same, and you change boats for every race. This puts the focus firmly on the sailing, not on the boat preparation. Joe's theory of how to do well in that type of racing was just as down to earth as his beginner sailing lessons. He boiled it down into a list of five critical sailing no-no's, which became a mantra for the Tufts National Championship team:

1. Don't be over the starting line early.
2. Don't be over the starting line late.
3. Don't foul out.
4. Don't hit the mark.
5. Don't capsize.

Bird's-Eye View

Managing your position on the race course and understanding "leverage" and the effects of wind shifts are central to tactical success. The biggest jump I made in my tactics was when I shifted my mental perspective from being "in" the boat to being "above" the boat. From above I can watch the race unfold and see the playing field—bounded by the laylines—so much more clearly. And from this overhead view, I can simply and easily understand the effects of wind shifts by mentally drawing an "even line" that is perpendicular to the wind direction (and that rotates with that wind direction). It's a bit like having the first-down line super-imposed over the video image of a football game.

I probably discovered this perspective when I started teaching racing to the kids at the Noroton Yacht Club Junior Sailing Program. On a chalkboard, the overhead view comes naturally. That's when I discovered the concept of *ladder rungs*. Sailing to a mark upwind or downwind requires "climbing" a ladder with rungs perpendicular to the wind direction. When the wind shifts, the ladder rotates, and instantaneous gains or losses are made depending on your leverage (distance of separation) across the course when viewed from above. Often, the best way to learn something is to have to teach it. And I've spent countless hours in front of the chalkboard and projector teaching this valuable concept of sailboat racing.

This bird's-eye view is so ingrained in my brain that when given the choice of watching a computer-animated America's Cup race from a cool perspective where the user can drive the virtual camera anywhere (like Google Earth), or from a simple two-dimensional view that is directly overhead, I'll always choose the latter. That's just the way my brain works.

Is the Race Over or Not?

My friend Larry Mialik has had a successful career at the highest level of two sports. He played professional football for the Atlanta Falcons and the San Diego Chargers, retired from that game, and got into sailing, where he won the America's Cup in San Diego as a grinder on *America*[3]. Larry—a native of the Midwest—is one of the most down-to-earth people you will ever meet. On a boat, he's the perfect teammate. His understated confidence helps everybody around him stay focused.

Off the boat, he can weave a yarn and tells plenty of stories—about football, farming, sailing, you name it. One of my favorites is this one. Larry was crewing for his friend Gary Jobson, another America's Cup winner, at a pro match race in Baltimore. The courses were short, and crisp boat-handling in the 44-foot sloops was essential for victory.

Now, keep in mind that at a match racing event, the pressure is high—with only two boats, you either win or lose. There's no in between. As a skipper, it's easy to get a little too overamped with all the pressure and say things to the crew that you really don't mean. I know; I've done it myself many times before. But I've never had a crew member do what Larry did in this particular regatta to put me back into focus.

Sailing off the starting line, Jobson called for a tack and began to turn the boat. But as the jib was getting trimmed in on the new tack, one of the other crew members who was hiking out got tangled in the jib sheet. Instead of filling crisply on the new tack and powering the boat forward, the jib was flapping, and the tangled crew member was struggling to extricate himself from the flying snake of the jib sheet.

Gary, who was pumped up for a perfect race, was crestfallen and announced to the crew, "That's it. . . . The race is over." Rather than try to verbally coax his skipper back to a good frame of mind, Larry used a much more subtle and powerful form of skipper psychology. Larry immediately stood up, grabbed the loose end of the jib sheet (now that the crew had unwrapped it from his legs), and started to coil it up. "What are you doing?" inquired his now exasperated helmsman. "You said the race was over," answered Larry to explain his midrace housekeeping, because when the race really is over and you're putting away the boat, you coil up the ropes. "It's not over!" yelled Gary.

Larry smiled as he trimmed the jib back in. The boat was back on course and at full speed, with the point well made. His helmsman was again focused on driving fast.

Killer

During my college years, our neighbor Mike Loeb, an Olympic 470 class champion, was a boat speed fanatic and drew inspiration from an antidrug slogan from the seventies—"Speed kills"—to name one of his boats *Killer.* In those days, Michael looked like he was straight out of Haight-Ashbury, with shoulder-length hair and penetrating eyes. He was so proud of his new boat and its name, that when a *Boston Globe* headline shouted "Killer on the Road," Michael cut it out and posted it on the passenger side of the dashboard of his beat-up old Chevy station wagon with its oversize 2 × 6-foot racks bolted to the roof.

One time on his way to Canada for a regatta—with *Killer* tied down on the roof—Mike stopped to pick up a hitchhiker. The guy was grateful for the lift until his gaze shifted to the newspaper clipping taped in front of him on the dashboard. He took one look at Michael and then another at the headline and quickly asked to be let out.

• • • • • • • • • • • RACER'S RULES • • • • • • • • • •
Dennis Conner

Dennis Conner—Mr. America's Cup—is a four-time America's Cup winner, successfully defending the America's Cup in 1974, 1980, and 1988 and winning as the challenger in 1987. He's won dozens of World Championships, including those in the ultra-competitive Star and Etchells classes. And he won an Olympic bronze medal in the Tempest in 1976. He was the first skipper of a Cup defender to be defeated in the 132-year history of the Cup, losing in 1983 to Alan Bond's wing-keeled challenger Australia II, four races to three—but he won it back four years later. I've sailed thousands of miles with "DC," and I learned something from him on every one of those miles. Here are a few of Dennis's racing rules:

1. Prepare.
2. Organize.
3. Know the boat.
4. Have a good idea of the level of the people you are working with.
5. Have a plan.
6. Encourage your crew to speak up.
7. Give them attaboys when they make the right decision.
8. Get the best people.
9. Attitude.
10. There are a lot of different ways to win.

Revel in the Routine

In my first America's Cup, as we got deeper into the trials and then the semifinals and the finals, the pressure was steadily mounting. As our winning continued and we neared the final rounds, there were more sponsors around the base, there were more family members sending in faxes and calling, and there was more pressure all around because the races were at the point where it was do or die—a best-of-seven series in the semis and the finals and then on to the Cup. It was then that I learned on a very big scale how athletes must effectively deal with pressure if they're going to keep their performance up.

A few years before, a sports psychologist had talked to the Olympic sailing team, which I was coaching. He said that even when the pressure gets high, we want to keep our arousal level at a very consistent intensity—no peaks and valleys just because one race is more important than another. In other words, we want to treat every race as if it's just another race. Ever hear that before? Well, believe me, that's pretty hard to do when you're sailing for the America's Cup and winning relies on you doing your job well.

But it's absolutely true—you do want to keep your arousal level and your performance steady, you really do need to treat it as just another race. The way you can do that is to revel in the routine. An America's Cup sailor has a routine—even on a race day. He gets up in the morning and goes to the gym to work out with the crew, has breakfast, and heads down to the base, where there's a certain amount of preparation that every crew member is responsible for. There's the normal routine that basically fills up every morning of an America's Cup race day. It's different, of course, for a grinder than for the navigator, but it's still a routine. And I started really just throwing myself into that routine and grasping onto that as this one bit of solid reality among the burgeoning fanfare.

Sure, I was soon going to be racing in the America's Cup, but I still had to make sure that the boat's batteries were charged on the instrument system. I still needed to make sure that my navigation equipment and spares were on board, and I still needed to make sure that I had the weather forecast and had gone through the briefing with Chris Bedford, our team's meteorologist. Those sorts of routine, mundane steps, which I had been doing for months and months, really kept me and my arousal level at a more steady level so that when the warning gun went off and we entered into the prestart, I had only a little bit of time to hyperventilate.

Hitting the Corner

In buoy racing, you learn to understand the concepts of leverage and risk-taking. It's pretty hard not to notice that many times on the first upwind leg of a race, the lead boat coming into the top mark appears to have come out of a corner. So why not get adventurous? It's like a gold mine out there, and when you're out at the corner you're like a miner because you're taking incredible risks separating so far from the fleet, sailing out to the very edge of the race course. If the wind goes your way, it's all good. If it doesn't go your way, it's all bad, and the amount that you gain or lose is directly related to how far you are across the course from your competition.

Sure, there's a time and a place for banging the corner and for rolling the dice. But it's like going to Las Vegas and putting all your chips down for one spin of the roulette wheel rather than playing a careful game of blackjack and counting the cards. Corner banging is a desperation move.

One of the most important things a sailor can do is to learn and to generate the discipline to avoid the tantalizing rewards of hitting the corner and separating from the fleet. The best sailors learn to apply a more disciplined tactical approach, where they play the odds in a much more conserva- tive fashion. In my early years in the Olympic 470 class, Dave Ullman was a master of this conservative sailing style, and I learned a lot watching him and his success.

If you do decide to hit the corner, however, there are the right and the wrong times to do it. You *don't* want to hit the corner, for example, at the beginning of a series or at the beginning of a race. Why? Because you don't need to win the first race of the series; you just need to finish in the top part of the fleet to have a good chance of winning the series. And why not at the beginning of a given race? Because if you get hopelessly behind, even if you're faster than the rest of the fleet, you're not going to be able to catch up. It's too risky. Later in the race, when the fleet is separated, taking a bit more of a risk is less dangerous because you already have a jump over a certain percentage of the fleet, and the points that you stand to lose if you're betting wrong go down.

In general, the only time I really try to wing it and hit a corner is in the last leg or last half of a race when I absolutely am clearly behind the competition and it makes good math- ematical sense to take the risk. You have to realize that the odds when you hit the corner are usually well less than 50 percent. Why? Because the majority of the boats tend to go the right way. So when you're splitting from them, you're already taking a high-odds choice. But there's a time and a place. And when you do come out of the corner and pass the entire fleet, it's a feeling like, "Wow, I'm so good." But really, you're not good—you're just damn lucky, and the truly great tactical sailors can recognize the difference.

Sail Care: Maintaining Your Boat's Engine

Sails are the engine of a sailboat, and there is no question that a fast engine—well tuned and operated correctly—is a powerful weapon indeed. Fast boats win races.

Probably my first experience of the value of having fresh sails was during my Olympic campaign in the Soling class. Before then, every boat I'd raced on simply had one suit of sails, which slowly (and sometimes not so slowly) degraded over time. But in our Olympic campaign we were working on developing faster sails with Tom Whidden and Peter Conrad of Sobstad Sails. We'd get a brand-new jib before a regatta, and it was like Christmas. Some of the new sails were measurably faster than our baseline inventory when flown in their designed condition. (In a Soling we usually carried two jibs on board, one for light winds and one for stronger.)

Over time, the stresses of hard time pulling the boat forward and exposure to sunlight and the elements cause sails to stretch and deform from their original shape. The drop-off in performance is measurable. A newer sail is simply closer in shape to the originally intended design. Once you find a fast sail design, a newer version of that same design will be faster than one that has significant sailing time on it. Of course, sail designers can make improvements in designs, too, but this is a hit-or-miss process.

To give you an idea of how valuable sails are to boat speed, in both the America's Cup and the Volvo Ocean Race—as well as all Olympic-class racing—the sails one can use in a regatta are limited by the rules. Furthermore, over the course of an America's Cup or a Volvo Ocean Race campaign, the number of sails (and wings in the case of the America's Cup) that a team can build and use is restricted. Otherwise the big-budget teams would have a huge advantage being able to design and test more sails and find a breakthrough.

Of course, new sails are expensive, and it doesn't make sense for most of us to be getting new sails for our boats all the time. We need to make our race sails last—hopefully for a year or more—which means taking good care of our inventory. You change your oil in your car every five thousand miles, right? Well, here are some ways I have found to best preserve these vital assets and extend the working life of your sailing engines.

- **Avoid flapping** Luffing or flapping a sail causes the sail material to lose its strength. Some America's Cup teams actually count the number of tacks a jib does. Why this obsession to detail? Because each time the jib is tacked, it flaps for a few seconds, weakening it. And with each tack, the leech also gets dragged across the mast and rigging, damaging the structure of the sail.
- **Avoid using the sail over its maximum designed wind speed** Even when properly trimmed, strong winds put undue strain on the sail and its fabric. The power of the wind goes up by the square of the velocity. So if the wind speed doubles from, say, 6 knots to 12 knots, the force imparted on every square inch of sail-cloth increases by four times! If your boat has sails for different conditions, such as a light-air jib and a heavy-air jib, you clearly don't want to put up the former

when it's blowing. In just a few moments it will turn into a balloon and never be the same. Some boats have just one sail for each position: for example, one mainsail, one jib, and so on. When that's the case, you can't shift to the heavy-air gear when the wind comes up. It's just a fact of life that if you sail in a windy location, your sails won't stay fast as long as if you sail regularly in a light-wind venue. But hey, it's fun to sail in strong winds, and that's just the price of admission.

- **Proper storage**   In the olden days, when sails were made of woven organic material such as cotton, proper sail storage meant avoiding mildew. Today sails are made of all sorts of ultrastrong synthetic materials that often can handle being put away damp but they don't like to be creased or crinkled. On smaller one-design and Olympic-class boats, sailors go to extremes to keep the sail cloth smooth by rolling the sails from top to bottom into cylindrical shapes rather than folding them. On bigger racing boats, where full-length rolling is not practical, the batten tension is eased off and sails are carefully folded to minimize the number of creases.

- **Trim your sails properly**   A sail's structure is engineered to take loads experienced when it's flying in its "normal" position. When I see a boat sailing with a batten missing in the leech of the mainsail, I cringe. That sail is getting unduly torqued because it doesn't have the stiff batten supporting the cloth where it needs it most. The cloth in that area will invariably degrade and begin to stretch—the sail is losing its shape. It probably won't break where it's been abused like this, but the wear and tear will add up to less performance.

When I was racing Etchells, the popular 30-foot keelboat class out of San Diego, the rules for many weekend regattas required that we leave our boats (which live all week on trailers in the parking lot) in the water tied to the dock on Saturday night. We were using a brand-new mainsail on Saturday and were planning on using it on Sunday, too. So we just left it rigged on the boom and rolled it up into a nice, smooth cylinder—no creases from folding. I took a couple pieces of rope to secure the sail to the boom for the night. And although I was very careful to avoid crunching the sail, I tied the ropes a little too tight. When we rehoisted the sail the next morning, you could see where those ropes had crinkled the sailcloth, cracking the resin in the fiber. The sail was still fast, but I had just aged the sail overnight by tying it down a little too hard. Every time I looked at it from that day forward, I could still see those marks and was reminded of my error.

The Inner Game

It all began during my college years at Yale, when sailing was arguably more a part of my life than it has ever been in the years since. I didn't live on or even near the campus. Instead my home was a twenty-minute drive down the freeway, at the Yale Sailing Center. My roommates included a future Olympic medalist and a 'round-the-world record-breaker. Sailing was the dominant feature in our lives, and I was looking for any new secret to further both my enjoyment of the sport and my performance in it.

One night I stayed at the house of my friend Gary Knapp on Long Island, where we were racing in a regatta. I looked on his bookshelf and saw a book with a fuzzy yellow tennis ball on the cover. Not knowing Gary was into tennis, I asked,

"What's this?" Gary's response was simply, "That's the best book on sailing that there is."

The book was *The Inner Game of Tennis*, and I soon discovered that Gary wasn't joking.

I picked up the book and flipped through the first few chapters. On the surface, it seemed to me that the book was about the mechanics of playing a better game of tennis. When I started reading more deeply, however, I realized that the book was actually about the *mental* aspect of the game of tennis—how to achieve the Zen of inner silence and perfection in a sport.

This concept resonated to me like a Jerry Garcia power chord. I soon bought my own copy of Timothy Gallwey's classic and devoured it inside and out, finding all sorts of parallels between his shared lessons from the tennis world and my world of sailboat racing. These were the days before "sports psychology" was a common buzzword, and this was my introduction to the concept that your state of mind—the mind of the competitor—can have a huge effect on your performance.

Sure, sailboat racing has its physical side (as I was enjoying on those cold, windy days hiking out in my Laser). But it is by and large a mental game. As Gallwey pointed out, your mind, your ego, and your expectations, fears, and hopes all could hamper your natural performance. A tennis analogy was to concentrate on the fuzz on the tennis ball coming at you. In this way, a properly trained and practiced athlete could make the perfect return shot without "judging" or "thinking" about anything but that ball—letting the body perform on its own without the aid of the analytical side of the mind.

The Inner Game of Tennis forever changed my sailing life.

I immediately strived to find ways to apply the lessons of the inner game to sailing. I became a walking advertisement for the book and the importance of the mental side of the sport. So much so that my very first published article was an

Inner Game–inspired piece titled "Zen and the Art of Sailboat Racing" for *Yachting* magazine.

Looking through this new prism, I realized that my very best races were ones where everything was flowing smoothly and effortlessly. These were times when I was making decisions swiftly and accurately, without judging whether a wind shift was good or bad—I just reacted to it faster than the competition, and soon was in the lead.

I also realized that there were many times when the pressure of expectations (we had a great college team vying for the national championship) or a negative mind-set kept me from reaching my ultimate level.

Part of the magic of the *Inner Game* has to do with being relaxed—with clearing your mind. That's why to this day I always try to find a piano (or a guitar) to play for a few minutes before leaving the dock. The process of making music clears my mind, reduces stress, and removes any mental obstacles that might be standing in my way.

A few years after I discovered *The Inner Game of Tennis*, my good friend and two-time Olympic medalist Jonathan McKee was my tactician aboard the fabled 12 Meter *Courageous*, sailing in the World Championships in Perth, Australia. The first day of racing was very windy, and the pin end of the starting line was highly favored—a challenging combination for a newbie 12 Meter helmsman. Jonathan recognized that my mental state was close to boiling over with all the stress of the conditions and my first time helming in the America's Cup arena.

So about four minutes before the starting gun, Jonathan provided a little mind therapy. He said, "Picture yourself at a concert. The drum solo has just ended and Jerry has walked back out onstage." With those few words, Jonathan took me far away from the pressures of driving an America's Cup contender and to the most mind-bendingly innovative phase of a Grateful Dead concert.

That was just what I needed. After that quick little mind trip, I was relaxed and able to focus on the task at hand—winning the pin end at the start and taking the lead over the twelve other 65-footers in the race. And that's exactly what we did. I'm convinced it was because I was able to remove the encumbrances of the mental pressure and stress that had built up in my brain.

In the decades since, the sport of sailing—and, indeed, most sports—have embraced sports psychology as an important element in achieving peak performance. The highly esteemed coach of the perennial NBA champion Los Angeles Lakers, Phil Jackson, is considered by many to be a guru in the mental game of his sport. His teams win not just on their physical domination of the sport, but also because of their mental domination of it.

Many of today's best sailors are intuitively great team psychologists. They use a variety of techniques to get their crew on the same page and operating in unison and at 110 percent. And those secrets, which I first was introduced to by a book with a fuzzy yellow tennis ball on the cover, are indeed applicable not just to sailing, but also to all aspects of life. Sometimes our minds can be full of gigantic distractions, each one competing for our attention. By using relaxation or mental imagery-focusing techniques to quiet your mind, you can indeed travel to a zone where you are focused fully on the task at hand, and your A-game will naturally emerge.

A few years ago, I ran across another interesting twist in my quest to achieve Zen-like peace in my racing. A literary agent of mine introduced me to a local psychiatrist—Dr. George Pratt—whom she had represented for his book *Instant Emotional Healing*. I met with George in his office at Scripps Memorial Hospital in La Jolla, and he explained how he and his colleagues were developing a new approach to psychological treatment. Dr. Pratt's system involved using a combination of Eastern and Western methods to help people get over neurosis, improve their performance, and clear themselves of a wide variety of other mental obstacles.

Sitting in his office, he illustrated the use of his techniques by, in just a couple of minutes, erasing my irrational fear of the dark. (It's never come back!) He then offered to create a race day routine on audiotape that could help me prepare my mind for the battle to come. The recording is about ten minutes long, and it involves following a particular sequence of repetitive self-affirmations while briskly tapping various parts of my hand and head.

In just a few months, Dr. Pratt's approach was put to the test.

I was calling tactics for Kenny Read aboard Dennis Conner's America's Cup entry *Stars & Stripes* in the 2000 America's Cup Trials. Talk about being in the hot seat! Our boat was pretty darn fast considering we were in a low-budget, one-boat program, and we were all of a sudden a dark horse with a real shot at making the semifinals. One morning before a big race, I decided to pull out my tape (alone—this is not something I wanted to show off in front of my team) and follow the routine.

On that particular day on the race course, my stress level was at an all-time low and the negative effects of any pressure I felt vanished completely. My mind was working swiftly, clearly, and with remarkable focus. I played that tape before every race day throughout the rest of the campaign, which ended in a quarter-final finish. And I have it on my iPod, which travels everywhere I go, even today.

$\backsim\backsim\backsim$

A Salty Sea Story

One of my favorite photo sequences of all time features Susan Daly—my crew at Yale—and me pitch-poling a Lehman dinghy in Chicago's frosty Belmont Harbor during the Timme Angsten regatta. The snow piled up on the mooring buoys in the harbor helped add to the frosty image.

The first photo in the sequence shows us sailing downwind in one of the twenty-odd races we sailed over the course of the three-day regatta. In the next photo, we are blasted with a big puff. Now, those Lehman dinghies don't plane—they nose-dive—so the next photo captured the scene as Susan and I quickly scooted to the back of the boat. But the bow kept plunging, water pouring in from the front. The second-to-last picture in the sequence is our blue-and-yellow sailing boots pointed upward as the boat completed its "endo" and we were catapulted into the icy water.

The final picture in the sequence is of the Chicago Yacht Club's crack rescue team hoisting our boat out of the water with a small crane mounted on a chase boat (those Lehmans were no strangers to the capsize). Meanwhile, out of frame, Susan and I were rushed back in a Boston Whaler to the clubhouse (only a few hundred yards away) where we jumped straight into a hot shower—sailing clothes and all. We quickly changed into dry clothes and sailed the next race.

The annual Timme Angsten regatta, held on Thanksgiving weekend, was the last major college regatta before racing shut down for the winter in the North. It was often frigid, and consequently one had to employ some rather unique techniques for the regatta. Since Lake Michigan is fresh water, when the temperature turns below freezing, you know what happens: it turns to ice. And if the wind chill is below zero, your water-soaked mainsheet freezes while you are sailing the five-minute upwind leg. So when you reach the windward mark, just when you want to ease out the mainsheet and bear away, it resembles a Popsicle more than a rope. There's no way it's going to fit through the tiny pulley on the boom and ease out when you turn to go downwind.

To avoid an ice-induced capsize, we would do a bit of creative preparation before leaving the dock prior to each race. We'd take our bailers (modified gallon milk jugs that we used to scoop the water out of the bottom of the boat) and fill them with some of the rock salt kept in barrels around the dock to keep everyone from slipping off the docks and into the water. Then we'd go into the bathroom and top up the bailer with steaming hot water from the sink. The chemical reaction that ensued was spectacular. When we got back to the boat, we carefully soaked the mainsheet in this bubbling concoction so it would not freeze. We'd then pour any remnants into the bilge of our dinghy to keep it from skimming over with ice and head out for our race.

The only problem is that I have a bad habit of putting the mainsheet in my teeth to facilitate trimming it in. And man, did it taste awful!

~~~

Always Carry a Knife

Close your eyes and picture a sailor—okay, I know, you've got Johnny Depp doing his pirate shtick in your mind's eye. Is he carrying a knife? You bet. And for good reason. All sailors work with ropes, and sometimes those ropes need to be cut in a hurry. So even modern-day sailors should follow the traditions of the olden days and carry a good, sharp knife with them at all times.

That lesson hit home many years ago when a hurricane brushed past my home waters of Long Island Sound. Outside the harbor it was blowing more than 30 knots out of the east, and although we canceled sailing class (I was teaching junior sailing at Noroton Yacht Club), the wind and waves were calling me. So my friend Andy King and I headed out in our

Lasers for some real heavy-air training in big waves. It was late August and the water was warm—we had a great time. After a nice, long session (where we capsized many times), the wind was building to a solid 35 knots-plus and we were headed back in. Suddenly we spotted another friend, Steve Hicks, having trouble in his two-man 470-class dinghy. His capsized boat had turned turtle, and he couldn't get it back upright.

We couldn't help him immediately—we had our hands full with our own boats—so we sailed back to the dock and I left my boat tied up and jumped into Andy's Laser for the rescue mission. We got out to the turtled 470 and I dove in the water and swam to the boat. With my help we were able to right the boat, but by then the wind had picked up even more and we needed to drop the mainsail and sail under jib alone to get the boat safely back to the dock.

After being flipped for so long, however, the halyard rope tails were hopelessly tangled. We had to get the sail lowered in a hurry, as we were drifting down on some rocks. Steve reached into his pocket and grabbed his trusty pocketknife and quickly sliced the rope halyard tails. The mainsail came smoothly down—just like that. Without that knife, the end of the story might not have had such a happy ending.

On that day I recognized that a good sharp knife (it does no good if you can't cut through the rope) should be easily accessible on every boat.

But what if the boat isn't your own? I was recently sailing with TeamOrigin—a British America's Cup Challenge team—in a regatta in Italy. We were sailing in a race where the 85-foot IACC boats were provided by the organizers. At the leeward mark in the final race, we had a major problem during the spinnaker takedown. It soon became clear that we were not going to get the spinnaker back on board the boat, so the call was made to cut it free. The spinnaker halyard and tack ropes were released cleanly. But as the spinnaker sheet was running out, the tail of the rope tangled around the foot of our jib trimmer, Mike Mottl. As the spinnaker landed in the water, it turned into a giant sea anchor, with all of its stopping force transferred directly to the rope wrapped around Mike's leg. Luckily a knife was handy on board and the sheet was cut before Mike's leg suffered serious injury.

Always carry a knife on a boat.

• • • • • • • • • • • RACER'S RULES • • • • • • • • • •
Roy Disney

The late Roy Disney was well known in the business world as a senior executive and former vice chairman of the Walt Disney Company, which his father Roy and uncle Walt founded. But Roy's greatest love was his sailing, and I had the pleasure to sail thousands of miles with him and his loyal team. Roy's boats (all named Pyewacket*) set several sailing speed records, including the one he coveted the most: the Los Angeles to Honolulu Transpacific Race monohull record, which was set on his 86-foot* Pyewacket *in July 1999 (7 days, 11 hours, 41 minutes, 27 seconds). Here are some of Roy's Disney's racing rules:*

1. Anyone can have a great idea—listen to him or her.
2. Have fun.
3. Persistence pays.

• •

Just for the Fun of It

Things can go wrong—on a race course, and in your life. Sometimes your decisions and actions are the causes of the problem, but sometimes the cause is outside of your control.

Dwelling on your misfortune is unproductive and can keep you from remedying or improving the situation. In a race, when the competitive juices are flowing freely, it's all too easy to succumb to a bit of self-pity at the worst possible moment: when you need to be thinking clearly and figuring out how to get out of the hole you're in.

Manton Scott was a brilliant young prodigy, arguably the most talented sailor of his generation. He won the Sears Cup (U.S. National Youth Championship) and was at the forefront of the new Olympic 470 class when his life tragically ended in 1973, at age twenty-one. Manton was rolling his 470 and trailer through a parking lot to the launching ramp when the mast hit a power line and he was electrocuted.

Although Manton grew up nearby, I never knew him—he was a few years older than I and light-years ahead of me in his sailing career when it ended all too soon. But one of his mantras sticks with me to this day. When something went wrong in the race and Manton found himself back in the pack, he told himself, "Okay, here we are. Now, just for the fun of it, let's see how far back up in the fleet we can get by the finish."

In case you missed it, Manton's operative word was *fun*. He knew that human nature is such that we tend to perform better when we are having fun.

⌇⌇⌇

The Art of Steering

Steering a sailboat is one of the most sensual things you can do in life. I remember as a kid first learning how to sail and going out on a windy day and realizing that the person steering the boat has control over a wide array of factors, including speed, whether you capsize or not, and which way you go. It's arguably the most fun thing you can do as a sailor. Sometimes it's incredibly easy—picture a lazy day slowly drifting across a lake—and sometimes it requires every single ounce of your sharpest concentration just to survive. In a race, the helmsman is focused on maximum performance and how to steer fast.

I truly believe that being a good helmsman requires both an artistic talent and a subjective skill of just feeling the waves and the wind, in addition to the technical skills of good seamanship. I remember sailing across the Gulf of California on the Santa Cruz 70 *Evolution* several years ago in an ocean race to Puerto Vallarta, Mexico. The fourth day out, we were on the final stretch with fewer than twenty-four hours to go to the finish line. The winds lined up perfectly, the spinnaker was set, and we were going at top speed. And if that wasn't good enough, it was warm and windy—T-shirts and shorts weather—and we had a steady mist of spray over the deck from the blazing bow wave. Ideal sailing conditions, paradise.

My friend Jonathan McKee was driving and I came up on deck with a cup of coffee to start my turn on watch. Jonathan was doing what, to this day, was the best job I've ever seen of high-speed steering in waves. He was completely in the moment and in the flow with the waves and the power of the wind and the boat—it was just a beautiful thing to watch. As I sat there on deck drinking my coffee, I tried to get inside his brain and watch the waves ahead and feel the heel and forces on the boat. I tried to anticipate how he would react with the wheel—"Okay, he's going to turn a little bit right now or he's going to turn a little bit left"—and he continued to amaze me with the small decisions he made. It's a joy to see someone steer a boat well, whether you're doing it yourself or you're just enjoying the ride.

I've learned that when it comes to steering, less is usually more. We all learn to steer by the feedback we get from a bunch of sensory inputs, including the angle of heel, the look of the sails, the telltales on the luff of the jib, and, if the boat is so equipped, the instruments. But when conditions are tricky—especially in light air and very big leftover swells, the conditions routinely experienced in my home waters of San Diego—the sails are being whipped around by the mast and the apparent wind is shifting radically. In these conditions, if you tried to steer the boat to keep the telltales flowing smoothly so that the sails are always at the correct angle of attack to the wind, you'd be using the rudder all the time. Unlike smooth water conditions, you have to just accept that the boat is not always going to be pointed in the perfect direction relative to the wind. Remember: the rudder is not just a steering device, it's also a brake any time you turn it away from the water flow. Of course, it's often a necessary evil to use that brake to turn the boat, but always be aware that there is a price to pay each time you use the rudder to alter your course.

At a recent Etchells World Championships in San Diego, I became aware of an invaluable steering technique that I probably had been using unconsciously for years. It involves focusing on a specific point on the horizon to help you steer straight. That may sound funny and even obvious if you've never sailed, but with all the forces above and below the water trying to turn the boat, keeping a steady course is not always so easy. A landmark on shore is the best reference, but if the horizon is out to sea, a cloud (remember, though, that they tend to move) or a star (they move, too, but a lot slower than a cloud) can provide short-term guidance.

Here's how it works: Let's say we're sailing upwind. First I get the boat grooving along on a course where it feels pretty good with the sail trim and the angle of heel, and then I focus my eyes on the horizon and say to myself, "Okay. Where am I going? I'm just going to keep steering straight at that point for one . . . two . . . three seconds. I'm not going to keep looking at all these other inputs that are going to be constantly changing because the swells are causing short local shifts. I'm just going to focus on steering straight." And in doing so, it means I'm not concentrating on steering to keep the jib tell-tales streaming straight (as I would in smoother water), which also means I'm not using the rudder motion to slow the boat and chase the randomly shifting breeze caused by the big swells. And then after a two- or three-second cycle, my eyes will go back to the telltales or I'll consider the feel of the boat, and maybe make a small steering correction. But it definitely quiets the steering motion when you lock into a visual landmark—and it can be very, very fast.

A similar steering approach can be applied on a windy power reach on a big keelboat. When the boat's all heeled over and on the edge of rounding up and wiping out, it's a very physical time to steer. It can be exhausting. After fifteen or twenty minutes on some boats, you're ready to hand over the helm. Despite the fact that it's a very physical workout, the natural tendency is to try to steer the boat aggressively and use your strength to keep it going fast. But a friend of mine taught me in the Fastnet race in England years ago that generally in those conditions it's best to find the right angle of the helm—either the wheel or the tiller, which keeps the boat tracking with a consistent heel angle on an average straight course—and just lock the helm, focusing on keeping a constant pressure on the rudder with minimal steering adjustments.

These techniques are hard to explain, but once you open your senses and get a feel for all the effects of rudder motion, you will get the idea. They're easier to "feel" than to see. Just remember that the rudder is a brake anytime it's used in a turn, and *any* turning motion slows the boat. It may be for the greater good and that deceleration is worth the course change you're making. But using the rudder just for the sake of being strong, or chasing a random wind shift, is guaranteed to slow your boat.

Adrift

Although the popular image of sailing is beautiful winds, sunny skies, and gentle whitecaps, coupled with a boat charging along with foam on its bow and wind filling its sails, in reality most sailing is done in light air and sometimes almost no wind at all. That's what we call drifting—when there's less than two to three knots of breeze and you're trying to eke whatever tiny bit of speed you can out of the little wind there is. It's slow. It can be frustrating. But it's also part of sailing. And the sooner you accept it for what it is and learn the skills you need to enjoy and go faster during the slower moments of sailing, the better off you are.

One of the most popular long-distance races in the world is the Newport Beach to Ensenada Ocean Race. The course is about 120 miles, and it's usually a short twenty-four-hour race. Hundreds of boats do it. One year I was on a 52-footer named *Pendragon*. As we were coming into Ensenada Bay near the end of the race, the wind just shut off. It was very, very light and the last eight miles of the race were sailed in drifting conditions. Little spots of wind would hit the water periodically, and you'd be sailing along at two or three knots for five minutes, and then nothing.

The lead boats—six of us—were going at about the same speed as we converged in the bay, all vying for the first-to-finish honors. One of them was Dennis Conner and his 60-footer *Stars & Stripes*, and there were a few Santa Cruz 70s and us, in our 52-footer. It was just after dawn, the sun was coming up, and you could almost taste the margaritas and tacos waiting for us on the dock. But first we had to finish the race, and at this point it was all about who was going to drift faster and spot the wind better than the others.

Part of good drifting tactics is to find your own private puff of wind, and everybody was trying to do their share of that. In those conditions, it often pays to haul a crew member up the rig to get a better perspective on where the wind is and isn't. Since any sort of wind creates ripples that look like dark patches on an otherwise glassy sea surface, it's pretty easy to spot where to go from up there. But the puffs can evaporate by the time you crawl your way over to take advantage of them.

But another part of winning when things get slow is maximizing the power from what little wind there is. In that race, we were all trying different techniques to do that, and at different points in this three-mile minirace up to the finish line each of us was in the lead for a short time. We were employing the usual techniques to gain boat speed in these conditions, including shifting the crew weight on the low side to try to heel the boat as much as possible to leeward. By tipping the boat to leeward, you let gravity force the sails into their designed shape. Then any air molecule that happens to be going past at least sees an airfoil and provides some propulsion. And the wind spotter's weight up there in the rigging also will help heel the boat.

Another trick is to move your crew weight as far forward in the boat as possible, especially on a bigger keelboat, where you should encourage a real party up on the bow. Because boats are normally narrower in the bow area, in the front, and wider in the transom, crew weight on the bow will reduce the wetted surface and the drag on your hull. By tipping the bow in and getting the weight forward as well as to leeward, you are reducing the drag of the hull as much as possible. When a puff does arrive, the frictional resistance of the hull in the water isn't holding you back as much. Interestingly, when the wind is up and the boat is ripping along on a reach, you want to move everyone to the windward side at the back of the boat to keep the bow out of the water (the heeling causes the bow to dig in) and to get the boat planing along on the flatter, wider surfboardlike shape of the back part of the hull. You normally have your biggest sails up in light air, but when it gets really, really light, the big headsail is actually a detriment because the air molecule that starts at the front of the sail and is supposed to go all the way to the back—providing that nice aerodynamic lift that helps to push the boat forward—loses its gumption and just stops. So at times when the wind was really shut off and boat speed was below two knots, we shifted down to our drifters, our smallest light headsails, which in *Pendragon*'s case was our spinnaker staysail. The smaller jib has a better chance of harnessing what little energy there is in the wind.

Finally, when there *is* a puff of wind—even if your destination is upwind (or downwind)—you should put the boat on a reaching course first. Don't try to point right up close to the wind. Instead, ease the sails out a bit and bear away while you try to build speed. Big keelboats can be very heavy. The keels are made of lead, and part of the game is to get that mass moving, building its inertia. And since in light air a close reaching course is the fastest point of sail, you want to accelerate at this angle. Once the mass of the boat gains momentum, even when the wind shuts off, your boat will coast a little while longer.

But in this particular race, right near the finish line, Dennis Conner started to employ a completely different technique than bearing the boat away from the wind and trying to build sailing speed in the anemic wind. DC realized that there was a big leftover swell. It was a good surf day on the beach somewhere, and because of the swell, the sails were flopping around. So he just turned his boat and pointed it straight at the finish line. He disregarded the random little puffs of wind, and he just let the wave motion flap the sails back and forth. While the rest of us were trying to "sail" at really wide angles to build speed with what little breeze there was, Dennis took a course straight at the finish line. By the time we recognized that his technique was working, Dennis had the lead and he simply traveled a shorter distance, using the kinetic energy of the waves pushing the sails back and forth to flap the boat forward like a bird pumping its wings. So even though we had all been following the classic rules of drifting technique, Dennis taught us a new one.

A word of warning: The racing rules prohibit using your body weight to rock the boat (which can be really fast in light air on a centerboard boat). But Dennis was using the waves, not his crew weight, to rock the boat, and that is permitted.

Local Knowledge: Handle with Care

Local knowledge—the understanding of local wind and current conditions and marine-related features—has for centuries been a cherished commodity, and sometimes a highly guarded military secret. In the days of the square-rigged tall ships the British navy would bring a local Portuguese pilot on board to help the ship's captain avoid obstacles such as reefs and sandbars or to take advantage of unique local conditions such as tides and winds. The same applies today. Everywhere you go, there are little nuances in the local conditions that can make a day sail or a cruise go smoother, or help a sailboat win a race.

During the summer months in most coastal places where we sail, there is a thermal-influenced breeze that blows in from the ocean during the afternoon hours. It's called the sea breeze effect, and it features a cool wind blowing from the cooler water to the warmer land. During the course of a sunny day, the land usually heats up faster than the water, with maximum heating occurring in the early afternoon. This temperature difference fuels an atmospheric engine that sucks the higher-pressure cool air over the water into shore. Depending on the actual temperature difference and the local geography, however—such as points or bays on a coastline—an afternoon sea breeze can have markedly different characteristics in different parts of the world. The way the sea breeze builds in a particular area—the direction it comes from, how it shifts with the passage of the sun, how it bends around points or funnels between two headlands— is replicated on many days in the summer months. And since understanding the way the wind shifts and where its puffs and lulls are located is crucial to winning races, this sort of local knowledge can be invaluable.

Part of local knowledge is actually just plain old micrometeorology or micro-oceanography—understanding the changes of the ocean, the current flow, or the wind flow based on small-scale features. So a really serious racer or cruiser is going to study the nautical charts that show the underwater topography to get a feel for how the current will flow and for how the prevailing wind might be affected.

If you're going to do a regatta in an area you're unfamiliar with, it helps to talk to the top local sailors to try to unearth some of the local conventional wisdom. For example, "It always pays to go to the left in the morning and to the right in the afternoon." Or, "If the wind is to the right of 210, then you've got to bang the right corner." You don't necessarily have to follow these general local rules, but you'll know what's in the heads of your competition. Local knowledge can actually be a handicap, because once you have local knowledge, you tend to apply it when other factors are more important. This is a big error. An expert sailor is going to have a healthy skepticism for any sort of local knowledge—at least understand that it rarely is 100 percent correct. Some of the most frustrated people I've ever seen on a boat are the local "experts" who say, "Peter, you've got to go this way because it always works," and I, using everything that I see, decide to go the other way. Sometimes I'm right and sometimes I'm wrong, but you've got to use more than just the age-old way of doing things. You've got to use your brain and keep your eyes open, too.

A great example of how dangerous it is to blindly follow local knowledge is racing on San Francisco's city front. In the summer months, the westerly breeze sucks in through the Golden Gate Bridge, providing relatively steady winds on a race course that also features incredibly strong (up to four or five knots) tidal currents. Over decades of racing, the local knowledge has developed into some pretty tried-and-true strategies that work for the different states of the tide. But a few years ago, Larry Ellison and Ernesto Bertarelli staged an exhibition match race series in their two IACC boats. Now, with their 14-foot-deep keels and 115-foot-tall masts, these boats are a lot different than the smaller, slower boats that had been sailed when the city front's local knowledge was developed. The locals were amazed and shook their heads knowingly when these pro teams did not short tack their way up along the shore in an adverse tide, as was the golden rule for the Bay. But these crews were doing exactly the correct thing for the IACC boat. Had they followed local knowledge in those big boats, they would have risked going aground and losing huge amounts of distance with every tack. For those particular boats, it was more advantageous to sail in stronger adverse current than strictly follow the local knowledge rules.

It is also important to appreciate that wind doesn't always act the same—even in exactly the same place with roughly equivalent conditions. There will be small variations in the meteorological forces that will affect how even the most consistent local feature occurs, and you have to be ready for those small differences. Don't get me wrong: there is a big advantage in getting to a venue early and doing your homework—both by talking to the locals to learn their tricks and getting out on the water and using your own powers of observation to see how the winds change.

An America's Cup team collects data from an array of private weather buoys and weather boats on the race course, records it, and then tries to model it with complex computer programs to develop their own local-knowledge rules. At the Cup in Valencia, Spain, in 2007, all the teams jointly funded the same weather buoy program and shared the buoy data information among themselves. But every team still had its own in-house meteorologist to analyze the data. And on race day—and on the many days leading up to it—the serious teams also had their own motorboats with really good sailors on board that would go out to specified locations equally spaced around the race course, throw out a sea anchor, collect data, and make visual observations.

They knew that there's nothing more valuable than local knowledge coupled with the open eyes of an observant sailor.

✺✺✺

Sailing at Night

The first time you sail at night is truly a remarkable experience. It's incredible when you get out in the open ocean on a clear night and are surrounded by a hemisphere of stars overhead. But even if you're sailing in a populated area where there are lights onshore and plenty of reflections on the water, everything is just so new and different. It's beautiful.

I love racing at night because of the extra challenges and opportunities it provides. Nighttime hours are when big gains can be made, because it's harder to sail well at night. Boat speed is less consistent, and tactical decisions are made more slowly. If you stay alert, concentrate more, have better skills, work harder, and are well organized, the rewards can be significant. In the daytime hours when the sailing is easier, it's hard to make those same gains. In fact, that's a great general rule in any race, day or night—the more difficult the conditions, the greater the opportunity to make big gains on the competition.

Being able to operate effectively on a boat at night, however, requires some new skills and practices. One of the most important is gaining your night vision, which requires keeping everything on deck as dark as possible—no unnecessary lights. Be sure you've got a blackout cover that goes across the companionway (the stairs going down to the cabin), which is often lit up by the crew below deck. If you must use lights on deck or down below, use as few as possible because it takes some time to regain your night vision, which you lose as soon as your pupils contract in the light. Whenever practical, use red-color lights instead of white lights—they don't cause as much night blindness, yet provide sufficient illumination for most tasks.

On deck, the crew should use flashlights as infrequently as possible. If it's a dark night with no moon, you are going to need to use lights from time to time to check your sail trim, run rigging, and prepare for setting new sails or making a maneuver. But it's important that the crew using the light keep the direct beam of their light away from the eyes of the sail trimmers and the helmsman, who are concentrating on sailing the boat fast. Keep the beam pointed forward and away from this "speed team" and use as dim a light as is practical. Mountain-climbing LED headlights that you wear strapped to your head are ideal because you can use both hands to prepare things and keep the beam aimed right at your work area. If you do splurge for one, make sure it has the red lens option so you use white light only when the dimmer red light simply won't cut it.

Almost every boat has two sets of built-in lights on deck: the instrument lights and the running lights. Running lights— aka the nav lights—are the red and the green bow light and the white stern light required by law to be lit during nighttime hours on all boats. There's a legal sector that the red and green bow light must transcribe from straightforward to basically two-thirds of the way back in the boat, but you shouldn't see the direct glow of the bow lights back in the cockpit or at the helm. If these bow running lights are particularly bright, or if there are sails or a bow pulpit or other pieces of rigging in front of the lights, they will reflect back very brightly, affecting the night vision of anyone looking forward. If reflection is a problem, get creative to try to minimize it. You can paint the bow pulpits flat black or you can wrap dark tape around the bars so the reflection doesn't look like a disco light show in the waves.

The other set of built-in lights most boats carry is the instrument lights. All sailing instruments are lighted red or green to make them easy on the eye at night, but you'll want to keep them as dim as possible while still being able to see them easily. As the sun goes down you will need to turn on the instrument lights to their max brightness, and as dusk fades to dark, you'll want to start dimming them.

Also, as the sun's about to go down, I have the crew put tape—usually electrical tape—on the active sheets for all the sail controls as a trim reference. Then, for example, if the spinnaker collapses at night and you trim in the sheet to refill it, you've got a physical target to ease it back to once the sail is full and you are back on course. These tape marks will help get your sail trim back in the ballpark very quickly after any disruption. Of course, don't rely *solely* on the marks. Unless the moonlight is very bright, from time to time the trimmers should use a flashlight to periodically check on the telltales and other visual trim aids and make changes accordingly.

When sailing upwind or close reaching, some people like to watch the telltales on the leading edge of the jib (as is common in daylight hours) even at night. If you have a telltale window on the luff of your jib, you can mount a flashlight on the windward foredeck stanchions to point up at the telltales. The downside of this technique is that it affects night vision, so I only do this if it will really help my team's steering on a given night. With nighttime visibility so limited, the helmsman is going to have to rely on other inputs to stay in the groove. These include the "feel" of the boat (especially the pressure on the rudder and the angle of heel), the sailing instruments (especially wind angle), and the compass. Just steering a straight course can be quite challenging when it's really dark. You'll learn to scan the horizon for any sort of visual guideposts such as the stern light of a boat up ahead, a star in just the right place off the forestay, or even the edge of a cloud (which, sadly, remains lined up for only a short while).

The moon is a big factor in night sailing. If the moon is up—half moon or larger—there will be enough ambient light for you to use fewer flashlights, if any at all. Once your eyes acclimate to the darkness, you'll be able to see the sails easily. And on a night such as you'll encounter sailing across the Pacific on the last couple of nights of a Transpac race from the West Coast of the U.S. mainland to Hawaii, you'll experience the majesty of beautiful trade wind clouds that light up as the moon shines through them. On those sorts of nights, it's actually quite bright, with shadows on the deck— even in the dead of night. Those are some of the most magical nights that you'll have out on the water. But as soon as the moon goes down and it goes dark, it gets very hard to steer and harder to hold a steady course. Believe me: the moon is your friend at night.

Keeping you and your crew alert at night can be very difficult, especially on the first night or two of a longer race when our internal clocks are not yet shifted over to the rhythm of a watch system. Here are a few general rules that I try to follow to help my performance at night:

- **Charge your batteries** Be well rested with a charged-up sleep quota before the race starts. Make sure you get a good night's sleep two nights before the start of the race.
- **Caffeinate** Make sure you have a system for anyone on the crew to make hot coffee or tea for the crew. If only one person knows how to operate the stove or the coffeemaker, your crew will go wanting at the most important time: the beginning or middle of the watch.
- **Dog your watches** There are a host of different watch systems that work, but it's better if they are designed so the night watches are shorter than the day watches. I also prefer the rotation-type watches where only one or a small group of people switch every time step rather than the simple A/B system where 50 percent of the crew switches at every watch change.
- **Communicate** By talking to your on-watch crewmates, you stay more in the game and also prevent them (or you) from succumbing to drowsiness.
- **Don't be a hero** If you are doing a job such as driving and starting to feel like you are losing the edge, switch out. Move around a little, go put the kettle on the stove, or grab a snack.
- **Monitor** In daylight hours it's easier to assess your boat's performance. At night, it takes work to keep track of your gains or losses. Use a handheld bearing compass and a notepad to keep track of all the boats visible around you.
- **Helpful handoff** Watch changes can be disruptive and a common time for performance to slip. When it's

your turn to go below and catch some z's, take time to fully brief the oncoming watch before you abandon them on deck. Remember, they may be sleepier than you. Discuss both tactical and speed-related subjects, including visual sail trim cues and performance numbers from the instruments.

～～～

The Physics of Sailing

When I was learning to sail, one of my favorite books was one I found on my neighbor's bookshelf: *Sailing Theory and Practice* by Czeslaw A. Marchaj. The book—essentially a textbook on the physics of sailing—explained in engineering/physical terms how sails, centerboards, keels, rudders, boat structure, and so forth all worked. When I got to Yale, Marchaj's nephew Conrad was a classmate of mine. We did a lot of college sailing together. His uncle is indisputably *the man* when it comes to the principles of sailing and the physics of sailing.

Although it's not absolutely necessary to understand the physics of sailing to sail a boat well, I personally find this knowledge to be quite useful. Every outstanding sailor I know understands more than just the rudiments of aerodynamics and the principles of lift—from America's Cup winners Dennis Conner (a carpet salesman) and Russell Coutts (an engineer), to the yacht designers, to the Olympic sailors. At the very highest level of the sport, most top sailors have taken the time to understand how their boats and sails work.

Understanding the science of sailing provides you with an advantage. And if you want to win, you'll want every advantage you can get. It really helps when changing gears on a boat. Most racers can reach the 98th percentile of performance in all but the most challenging of conditions. You've got the boat going fast, but you want to go that extra 2 percent. To do this you make really small adjustments to the way you steer or the way you trim the sail or the way the crew balances the boat, and these little changes can make all the difference. If you understand from your knowledge of airfoil theory, for example, that flatter sails are better for heavier air and fuller sails for light air, then you have an edge in making those tiny adjustments as the conditions change. And the physics of foils (wings) teaches us that a foil with a more-forward draft position is more forgiving—it can handle more variation in the angle of attack. This gives you a leg up when you're adjusting the luff tension of your sails or the sag of your headstay. Bottom line: when conditions are choppy, with the waves "bigger" than the wind, you'll do better with the draft in your sails positioned more forward.

If you take the time to learn about how a boat works, the science of fluid flow, and the principles of aerodynamic and hydrodynamic lift, you will become a better, more complete sailor.

• • • • • • • • • • • IN THEIR OWN WORDS • • • • • • • • • • •
Jonathan McKee

Jonathan McKee is one of our country's most talented sailors. Since graduating from Yale University (where he was an All-American sailor), Jonathan has raced a wide range of boats with success. He competed in the Flying Dutchman class at the 1984 Summer Olympics in Los Angeles and won a gold medal with his crew Carl Buchan. At the 2000 Summer Olympics in Sydney he teamed up with his brother Charlie in the 49er class to win the bronze medal. He's won world championships in a variety of boats and has been part of several America's Cup campaigns.

Be careful what you wish for!

The crew selection process is always a very stressful time in an America's Cup program. Two full teams of sailors get narrowed down to one group of first-stringers and another group of reserves. While everyone is important in their own way, from a personal perspective there is a big difference between being a starter and not, and it is quite a challenging time for the whole team.

In my last America's Cup, there were two crew selection choices that I really did not agree with. I was not sure they were based on pure merit, and my sense of fairness was disturbed. I had been pretty involved in many of the strategic decisions of the campaign, but I was not a direct party to the crew selection. When I heard of the choices, I immediately made my displeasure known to the team leaders. They were taken aback at my outrage, but in the end they reconsidered and changed the two controversial crew choices.

This proved to be enormously disruptive to the team. Obviously the two crew who were unselected were very upset, and many of the crew felt the process had been subverted. There was a lot of bad feeling, and a lot of angst by the management, which was a big distraction at a time when we should have been focused on winning the America's Cup.

In the end, I had to question whether I had done the right thing by objecting to the original crew choices. Maybe the crew was nominally better. But the price of this was a divided and upset team. So on balance, my actions probably hurt the team more than they helped it. At the time, I thought I was doing the right thing. But I let my sense of justice override the overall well-being of the team, and I learned an important lesson about always keeping the big picture in mind. After all, there is no "I" in team!

• •

◁◁◁

When to Hold and When to Fold

When things get tough out on the water, when do you decide to forge ahead, and when do you decide to retire? Once you're in really rough conditions, there's no getting out. Sure, you can always choose to simply turn around and surf back to shore, or take the course that puts the least stress on the boat, but if it's still blowing gale-force winds and twenty-five-foot waves, no matter which way you go you're still in dangerous conditions. That decision of whether to turn tail and go for the closest, safest port—or not—is something that really has to be made in the moment, considering the boat, the crew, and your best guess as to the most likely outcome from each alternative. Although the decision to drop out of a race can be a difficult one—you've committed fully to the race, after all—if you do your homework looking at weather forecasts, you can get a pretty good idea of how bad things might be.

I sailed on *Titan* in the 2007 Middle Sea Race in which George David's boat *Rambler* took almost 50 percent off the record in gale-force winds. The race course skirted dangerous shores, the weather was extraordinarily rough, and most of the fleet didn't finish the race—one boat sank. As we prepared for the race, we knew that a brewing low-pressure system would make the race interesting. The race starts in Malta, runs around Sicily, and returns to finish in Malta. You're in protected waters early on until you get through the Straits of Messina, and then you're out on the northern side of Sicily in more open seas. At that point—halfway through the race—was when this minibomb low-pressure system was expected to hit. Before the start, as each new weather model came through, the forecast kept getting worse and worse. The predicted winds kept getting higher and higher—sixty-knot, seventy-knot, and finally I saw one-hundred-knot winds forecast for the halfway point in the race, which I'd never before seen in any race I'd ever done anywhere.

I phoned the race committee before the start of the race and suggested that they postpone it, instead setting up a different, shorter course. The committee declined my suggestion, however, themselves suggesting that it was the responsibility of each boat to make the decision to go on or not. In my opinion, this wasn't just a cop-out, it also was a bad decision.

So we started the race and sailed hard. During the course of the first evening, we downloaded new weather files as they became available. Instead of getting better, things were looking like anything but. The latest weather file produced the worst forecast yet: hundred-knot winds for several hours, in an area where there was no easy port to run into. *Titan* wasn't set up for heavy, ocean-type racing in forty-knot winds (and no sailboat is built to sail in hundred-knot winds). *Titan* was configured for around-the-buoys and coastal racing—a lightweight, 75-foot carbon fiber sloop. We didn't have heavy weather offshore gear such as "lazy jacks" to help the mainsail stay in control if we had to drop it in an emergency. We didn't have a third set of reefs in our mainsail—it could be reduced in size by only 30 percent, not 60 percent. The mast was light. We had broken one check stay right off the starting line. So although we were an internationally respected racing team in a boat that was more prepared than 95 percent of the fleet, I didn't think we were in any way ready for the conditions the forecast was portending.

I conferred with the tactician Benny Mitchell, boat captain Scotty Bradford, and our sail maker Mike Toppa to get a consensus and then discussed things with our skipper—*Titan's* owner—Tom Hill. I told him that I didn't think that the boat could survive the race in one piece. I didn't think it was prudent to continue into the heart of the storm and recommended immediately withdrawing and sailing back to Malta. It was a tough call for Tom to make. He'd shipped his boat from the United States all the way to the Mediterranean to sail in this, one of the great ocean races on the planet. We were first or second in the race at the time on this great boat, and we'd never dropped out of any race before. But Tom has years of ocean racing experience, and he agreed with me. We told the crew that the race was over, turned the boat around, and sailed back into Malta that night—before the storm hit.

The next day we learned that the pro team on *Loki*—a near sister ship of *Titan*—had continued in the race and sailed around the northern side of Sicily, gotten slammed by the storm, broken their rudder, abandoned ship into a life raft, and called in helicopters to rescue the crew. As they jumped off, the crew had put out all their anchors with as much line as they could find. They hoped the anchors would hold, even with no one on the boat, until the storm abated and the crew could brave the big waves and get back to save it. But the anchor lines chafed through and *Loki* washed up onto the rocks and was destroyed.

My friends on *Rambler*—which *did* complete the course—have some great sea stories. Scenes from these stories include the following snapshots: all their sails lashed down except the storm jib, huge seas, surfing along, everybody down below except a couple people on deck because it was so dangerous. But they won the race and set a new record doing it. They had the same forecast we did, and their decision was to keep going. For them it was the right thing to do. *Rambler* was all pimped up for ocean sailing, having just won a rough transatlantic race. They were more prepared than we were for the near-hurricane conditions, and they were lucky. At one point at the height of the storm, their forward hatch blew off its hinges under the force of the huge waves crashing over the deck. Luckily the hatch fetched up on the mast long enough for the crew to grab it and jury-rig it back into place. Had they not gotten it back in place, they easily could have sunk in those conditions.

Normally, I'd be a bit jealous of friends who beat me in a race because I chickened out. But in this case, I'm simply happy they survived to set the record, and I'm sure we made the right decision for our boat.

Testing

Everybody wants to go faster out on the water, and some people will do just about anything to squeeze some extra speed out of their boat. Once you've got a good feel for your boat, you'll want to start experimenting with different setups and learn more about what your boat can and can't do. There's no question that actual racing is the best practice to develop all the skills necessary to win. But if you are at the point in your sailing where you really want to employ the scientific method to focus on a specific boat-speed component, a sailboat race may not be the best forum. This is because the enemy is not your perfect benchmark—they're doing their own random things. You might have a five-minute period where another boat is right alongside and being the perfect benchmark so you can experiment with some different technique, but it doesn't happen as often in racing as you'd like. Plus *they* may be changing things at the same time.

The traditional, Dennis Conner–style way of testing and trying new ideas—whether they be sails or equipment—is to use two boats sailing side by side and do long, organized tests with a defined start and ending point. The boats will line up about two mast lengths apart so neither boat directly affects the other's wind. When testing upwind the windward boat will set up almost abeam of the leeward boat. They'll sail along for four to seven minutes, with one boat being assigned to be the fixed boat—the trial horse—and the other boat testing the new sail or equipment. You can test going downwind in a similar manner but with a different lineup. When testing downwind, you usually start the test with one boat nearly dead astern of the other but far enough apart so that the wake and disturbed wind of the boats do not have an effect.

It'd be nice if you could test alone, just using your instruments. Unfortunately, sailing instruments aren't accurate enough to provide feedback to the level of precision you need. The problem is related to the challenge of keeping sailing instruments well calibrated. There are so many variables in measuring the wind, and the boat's speed and course, that it's virtually impossible to keep the instruments in tune all the time. Sure, the instruments will tell you if you're really out of the groove, but when testing, the differences we're looking for are so small that the only way to be confident of your results is when sailing against another boat.

Some people test with three boats, but that's just one more variable in the mix, and it gets that much harder to set up the testing lineup so that everybody has a fair lane. Although racing is the best way to learn and improve your sailing, there is a time and a place for two-boat testing. So take an afternoon, set up a specific goal, and run four to six tests just trying to achieve that goal. That will hopefully filter out any variations in the wind. But it takes incredible amounts of time and patience to be able to come to any significant conclusions because of the vagaries you're faced with out on the water. That's a part of testing you can't avoid, no matter how hard you might try.

How to Be the Ultimate Offshore Shipmate

A lot of younger sailors ask me what they can do to get noticed at the higher levels of the sport—how to earn a spot in a big program. Of course, success in small-boat sailing is probably the most direct route to getting noticed and invited onto a big boat or professional campaign, but you also need to build a reputation of being a good shipmate. And if you do get that golden opportunity to sail with the team of your dreams, you want to come across as being the ultimate shipmate so you'll be invited back.

What does that mean? Of course it means being a contributing member of the crew, thinking first and avoiding mistakes, following instructions and asking questions if you don't understand, and doing the jobs you are asked to do. It also means volunteering to do extra work. If a line needs to be coiled or if a sail needs to be folded, you're the first one up there helping out. When there is a sail change and they need some extra hands up on the foredeck getting wet and pulling the sail down, you go up and do it. When just sailing along straight, you volunteer to give others breaks doing the less glamorous grunt work such as grinding winches. Or when off watch, instead of winning the golden blanket award by being first in your bunk, you grab a bucket and sponge out the bilge—now, *there's* a thankless job. And even if you're just sitting on the rail, you hike out harder than everybody else— all the time. By example you're clearly showing that you are someone who is valuable on a boat.

When you're on a big boat—especially in a long race— you're crammed together with people and equipment in a pretty confined area. Everybody has to give up a little bit of their own personal space to make life comfortable and livable for everybody else. Down below deck on a big ocean racer, you want to keep all your gear in your bag, and keep your sea bag tucked away in the appropriate place. Don't leave your stuff all over the place. Keep it contained and within a small footprint. The term *shipshape* is no accident. Pack light and make sure your sea bag is smaller than average for the crew. Before your turn on watch, wake up early, put on the kettle, and offer up a round of hot coffee or tea to the guys on deck.

When you're going off watch down below, offer to put on the kettle and throw some snacks up to the team on deck. (A way to a sailor's heart is through his stomach!) Think about the other guys and make a mark on them with your can-do attitude and putting their comfort before your own.

The Racer's Edge

The key to getting a jump on the competition is keeping the playing field tipped in your favor. It's no secret that getting an edge in a competitive environment means being prepared. To do so in sailing requires the experience to know to prioritize what you should be working on. It requires the resources to be able to travel to where the best competition is and to buy and develop the equipment that's going to help you. And it means putting in the extra time necessary so you're just a little bit more prepared than the other teams.

One of the most dramatic examples that I've seen of the success that can be achieved by prioritizing and setting realistic goals was at the 2000 Olympics in Sydney. JJ Isler and Pease Glaser won the U.S. Olympic Trials in the 470 class but had not sailed together much as a team internationally. Their world ranking started out in the triple digits. But JJ and Pease both had previous Olympic experience, and they didn't panic and change a lot of things—they just stayed on track. They acquired the best equipment, and they set a training schedule that worked for them to avoid burnout. And they thought long and hard and made a list of their weaknesses, prioritized them, and then set out a plan to work on them. Just as important were the things that they agreed were not important to change. In the end, this team—which had never finished in the top ten of any international regatta in the previous four years—won the silver medal.

I think back to my days studying the habits and techniques of the best Olympic-class and small-boat sailors. Dennis Conner would always try to be the first boat off the dock on the morning of a race day. He may already have had the best-prepared boat, and the best crew, and the best sails, or whatever. But Dennis took it to the level where no stone was unturned. Following his example, I try to be out on the course an hour before the start. But by going out fifteen minutes before *that*, you have 25 percent more time to try to ascertain what the wind is doing, to get your equipment sorted out, and to shake off the cobwebs.

In college sailing, where you rotate boats every race or every other race, there is no advantage available in boat preparation. And in some ways, I still love that style of sailing, where we're all sailing dead-equal boats and it's all about what you can do when you get out on the water. Then the preparation is more your own knowledge and your ability to switch it on and bring your A-game when the preparatory signal goes, and less about having a magic boat.

The complete opposite of that style of racing is a development class like the Moth. The Moth is a super-cool one-man boat that flies with its hull completely out of the water, riding on a hydrofoil. This class is highly technical and all about being able to get your boat out of the water and flying on these hydrofoils. Technique and equipment are all-important there. You could be the best tactical sailor and have the best start and be going the right way in every race and you will finish dead last if you are not fast and have failed to spend the requisite time in the parking lot working on your equipment.

The sport is so diverse that you can pick the type of sailing that best suits your style. Some people enjoy the development and speed stuff—tinkering with their boats for hours to get an edge; others prefer the raw, tactical, split-second-decision sailing that is the hallmark of match racing and short-course dinghy racing. And some enjoy the big-boat, ocean-racing programs where big-team organization is rewarded and decisions made a year or more before the race (in the design and engineering phase) can make the difference.

Because of my college sailing background, a big part of me prefers the game when we all come equally armed to battle. I think that's why I get drawn into match racing and one-design racing more than the development classes. I just find that to be a really pure aspect of the game of sailing. There are no excuses out there—you're only as good as your last race.

◯◯◯

Naviguessing

Racing navigation has changed a lot since my early days of sailing when I plotted our boat's course by dead reckoning— taking bearings of lighthouses and buoys off the binnacle compass. Electronic navigation was in its infancy, with radio directional finders (RDFs) and LORAN providing sometimes very iffy fixes—hence the endearing title "naviguesser," which was commonly used back in the day. Now it's all about GPS, thanks to which everybody knows exactly where they are to within a few feet. The challenge in race navigation today is really gathering and communicating the information that will help the tactical team make good decisions. The computer is now a ubiquitous tool on board bigger race boats, but like at home, where you can waste away countless hours surfing the Web, it's easy to overrely on the computer to the detriment of your performance. To really take it to the next level and be effective as a navigator today, you have to be a contributing member of the sailing team on deck, too. That means continuing to do your job and being able to picture the race course and the what-ifs in your mind's eye even when you don't have a computer or a chart in front of you.

Sure, there are times when I'm glued to my computer screen down below deck in the "navigatorium," downloading weather files or analyzing them to find an advantage. But my navigation philosophy—especially for buoy races—is to be an on-deck, head-out-of-the-boat style navigator. And to do that you've got to have the information you need available on the sailing instruments. I'm very picky about exactly what information is being displayed on the sailing instruments to help me make better decisions, and it's one of the first things I tweak when I get on a new boat. I often set up different "pages" on the instruments so I or the crew can shift to the most important information at a particular part of the race.

Being a good navigator also means having the mental mathematical skills to be able to calculate in your mind's eye what effect a particular strategy might have. A common strategic conundrum, especially in long-distance racing, is that often the direct course to the mark isn't the fastest point of sail. Dennis Conner taught me a trick many, many years ago while we were sailing across the Gulf Stream in Florida. Let's say the destination is 60 miles away and you're pointing directly at it with no current—you are sailing the shortest distance. But sometimes by changing your course by turning away from the mark one way or the other by, say, 5 degrees, you can pick up, say, 10 percent more speed. So the VMG (velocity made good) to the destination is better by sailing off course for now, but it means sailing extra distance. Is that extra distance worth the speed/VMG gain?

First you have to determine how much extra distance you will be sailing. This geometric puzzle can be solved using sines and cosines—or by plugging the information into a computer (which we didn't have on board twenty years ago)—but Dennis had a trick to get very close to the answer without breaking out the slide rule. If the destination is 60 miles away and you're 5 degrees off course, when you sail those 60 miles you'll be 5 miles—1 degree per mile—away from the destination. So if the destination is 30 miles away and you're 5 degrees off course, then you're pointing 2½ miles away from the mark. That kind of mental geometry helps you to make decisions quickly and determine whether it's worth a particular course alteration. Of course, when you're making these long-term decisions, understanding and having a feel for what the weather is going to do is also important because one of the general axioms of navigation and racing is that the wind *will* change.

So if the leg is long enough, your strategy should be to sail the course that will get your boat closest to the mark as quickly as possible. If you have a good idea of how the wind will change, you can factor that into your routing. But even if you do not, you can bank on the wind changing somehow. This often means forgoing the most direct course in favor of a faster sailing angle, because you anticipate a change in the wind that will create a new strategic (and geometric) challenge. The next step is having the tools to be able to develop a guesstimate as to what the wind will do in the time you are on this particular leg. Then you plug that into the decision-making as to what course to take. If the wind is going to shift one way, you might be happy sailing off course on a faster angle, but if it's going to shift in the opposite direction, you may decide it's better to simply sail directly at the mark. However, rarely do you sail in a direct course, and it's deciding how far off course to sail and which way, to the right or to the left, at a tighter or broader wind angle, that is key in ocean-racing navigation.

A word of warning: if the leg is short, or if by some chance the wind doesn't shift, the most direct course will be the best.

That's why in short-course buoy racing, you don't usually employ such aggressive course changes in your strategy.

During an ocean race you can download weather files and use the computer tools on board to help develop these guesstimates. I'm personally very involved in developing the Expedition tactical and navigation software I use (www .tasmanbaynav.co.nz). But without good information going into the computer, it can be all garbage in and garbage out. Theoretically, if you plug in the course, the weather information, and the boat's predicted performance information (its polars), the computer will give you the ideal course to take. But the weather files are never exactly right, and your polars, even if you've taken the time to fine-tune them, are affected by what sails you have on board and the sea conditions. So when the computer tells you to go one way, you shouldn't follow it blindly. You should analyze the computer results to see how critical it is to take that exact course. And you may hedge your decision as to how much you split with the fleet—especially early in the race—based on how confident you are of the data you are using.

The longer races I rue the most are the ones where I had an incorrect hunch to split with the fleet, and I followed that hunch early in the race rather than hanging with the competition until there was a clearer opportunity to split and gain. Looking back, I realize that in those instances, it wasn't that I was feeling strongly about splitting. I was simply looking to hit a home run—to earn a navigational win. Well, there's nothing wrong with sticking with the fleet and making the crew win the race. Sure, many ocean races are ultimately won by a navigational decision, but even more are lost by an incorrect decision. The navigator should not feel that he needs to be providing miracles right and left—that's desperation tactics. Your boat's biggest weapon should be just being able to hang with the competition when there's no obvious navigational play and sail a little bit faster in exactly the same water they're in.

In a way it's like the having one superstar on a basketball team. They feel confident they can score every time they touch the ball, but ultimately the team is weaker if they depend on one person to always come up with the big plays. You've got five guys on the basketball court; use them all. It's the same thing in a sailboat race. There are times to take a flyer and follow your hunch. But sailing is the game of odds. Remember, nothing is absolutely certain out there on the water.

• • • • • • • • • • • **RACER'S RULES** • • • • • • • • • • •

Chuck Robinson

Chuck Robinson is president of CBTF Co. and M Ship Co., and he recently retired from being a board member of Nike and the chairman of Nike's Finance Committee. Chuck headed up a team that included Bill Burns, Matt Brown, and Peter Isler to create a radical new sailboat technology called CBTF (Canting Ballast Twin Foil). Since the first CBTF boat was built in the early 1990s, there have been a number of highly successful maxi boats (including Pyewacket, Morning Glory, Alfa Romeo, *and* Wild Oats*) that have employed CBTF technology. Here are Chuck Robinson's racer's rules:*

1. Take chances.
2. Innovate.
3. Do things differently.
4. Manage by self-induced crisis.
5. Tilt the playing field in your favor.
6. There's no reason to exist if you're not creating.
7. Refuse to overanalyze and overcalculate your decisions.
8. Share the wealth.
9. Know the level of risk you can absorb.
10. If it's worth doing, do it the best you can.

• •

ᏋᏋᏋ

Used-Car Salesmanship

The day before I left Perth after winning my first America's Cup, I had a lot to do, and we were on a really tight time frame. One of my personal tasks was to sell a car I had bought for our five-month stay in Western Australia. It wasn't anything special—just a fifteen-year-old Ford Falcon with an awful army-green paint job. It had roof racks on it and was mainly used to transport sailboards to the beach on our rare days off. My friend and teammate Duncan Skinner suggested that I could enhance its resale value with a bit of creative cosmetic surgery.

So I pulled the car into the *Stars & Stripes* team compound and put out a bunch of Magic Markers on a table next to the car with a sign that read AUTOGRAPH ME. Soon, most of the team along with some of our sponsors had signed the car—and as time went on each signature was getting bigger and more creative in its placement. As I took photos to document the signature frenzy. Duncan put a big US 55 sticker (*Stars & Stripes'* famous sail number) from the sail loft on the side of the beat-up car. When the "decoration" process was deemed complete, I went out to the gate of the base, where thousands of people were standing outside, wanting to get a glimpse of Dennis and the crew. Remember, this is all happening the day after we won, and I had twenty-four hours to sell the car.

So I yelled out to the crowd, "Anyone want to buy a car signed by the entire *Stars & Stripes* crew?" I did this about three times over the course of the morning as I was doing my chores like rinsing and packing up my navigation equipment. All of a sudden one of the security guards came up to me and said, "Hey, Peter, there's a guy out here that wants to take a look at your car." As it turned out, it was a car dealer from a town about a hundred miles south. He came in and took a look at this old beat-up old Ford signed by the entire crew. On the back, where it said FORD, Edsel Ford II (great-grandson of Henry Ford, who was in town because Ford Motor Company was one of the team's sponsors) had even written EDSEL to the left of the Ford badge on the trunk and placed the roman numeral II to the right of the badge. And so it was signed by a member of the family whose company had built the car, too.

Thanks to all the America's Cup frenzy, this old car had new legs, and we quickly consummated a deal. I sold the car for three times more than I had bought it for!

~~~

Choosing the Right Crew

Years ago, I did a seminar at Mission Bay Aquatic Center in San Diego, and among the instructors there that day were archrivals Dennis Conner and Tom Blackaller. Conner and Blackaller were fierce competitors in the Star class and in the America's Cup arena. Tom was a charismatic hip-shooting sail maker from the San Francisco area, and Dennis was a methodical, detail-oriented sailor from San Diego.

The subject came up about how to choose a crew. Both of them agreed on one thing: attitude over experience. Sure, you want people on the boat who have done the job before, know how to do it, and are the best in the world at it. But both Blackaller and Conner also made the point that when given the choice between an individual with a ton of experience and attitude issues and an individual with less experience but a really good attitude—easy to get along with and a strong work ethic—they would pick the person with the good attitude every time.

When forming a long-term team such as for an America's Cup campaign, you are building a group that will be working together for months or even years on end. You want people who have a positive attitude and who are going to be able to go through those long hours while working and playing well with their teammates. You can teach almost anyone with a good attitude how to do a job well, but you're never going to be able to fix a person who has ego issues or who isn't a great team player.

I've noticed that this is very much in play in the top racing teams that get put together by some of the guys I really respect most in sailing—guys such as Russell Coutts or Kenny Read. You rarely hear stories about one of their crew members running into trouble or getting fired because they did something wrong. Most of the high-level teams of which I've been a part are an amazingly nice group of people. In this league, a lot of the ballooning egos and interpersonal gamesmanship you often see in the amateur ranks go away. It's just all about working hard, racing the boat hard, and having fun. And winning.

Playing by the Rules

The sailboat racing rules were originally structured so that if you fouled, it was your duty to voluntarily admit that you were wrong and simply drop out of the race. And to this day, the sport of sailing is structured around a set of rules designed to be self-policing. Of course, the more competitive a sport becomes, the greater the temptation to cheat. But far and away the best sailors I've sailed with are a very honest and fair bunch. Sure, they push the rules as far as they can be pushed, but when the rule is black-and-white, they're black-and-white about it, too.

But some rules are so universally broken that new sailors to our sport start to get the impression that cheating is okay. That is bad for the sport. My current pet peeve concerns the lawlessness (in some big-boat fleets) around Rule 51, the Movable Ballast Rule. The rule clearly states that you're not allowed to move your unused sails (which are stowed down below) for changing trim or stability. A big racing boat such as the 75-foot *Titan* might have ten to fifteen sails in bags stored below-decks, and they're quite heavy.

Now, in some races, such as some of the around-the-world races, Rule 51 is specifically relaxed so that you're allowed to stack those sails on the deck. Teams design the deck layout so this valuable movable ballast can be loaded way out on the edge—right where the weight is most beneficial in keeping the boat from heeling. It's like having a dozen guys hiking out hard all the time. But in most sailing, and unless it's specifically changed in the Sailing Instructions for a given race, Rule 51 applies. That means that in the case of sails, you're only allowed to move a sail if you're going to pull it up on deck in preparation for hoisting it, or for some other reason unrelated to getting a performance advantage. These reasons might include bailing the bilge or digging out a sail that is underneath a stack. But you're certainly not allowed to move the sails down below from one side to the other when you tack just because that gets the weight to the high side where it's more efficient.

But guess what? A lot of boats *do* move the sails around down below for better performance, even though it's clearly illegal. I think it's done partly because, aside from being clearly faster, a lot of sailors don't realize they are breaking the rules. Others justify it under the "Everybody else is doing it—and there's no way we can get caught" rationale. The first guy I ever sailed with who made a point of making sure that that *didn't* happen was Dennis Conner thirty years ago. He made it very clear to his entire crew that he did not condone this cheating. At the time I thought, well, maybe he's just making an appearance to be honest in this less-important race because in the America's Cup he's doing all the super-tricky stuff. But I've sailed with him a lot over the years since, and believe me, when a rule is black-and-white, he is always on the white side. Some of his boats have had some incredibly tricky and clever stuff that really bent the rules. But Dennis always made sure not to break the rules. Dennis's integrity rubbed off on me.

When I see younger sailors start to move sails around down below, I'll have a word with them. I must admit there are times I've woken up from a nap and all the sails have been magically moved to the high side, and I didn't immediately turn us in to the referees (there are none in our sport) and demand that we drop out of the race. I'm certainly not perfect. But I feel a lot better when I'm playing by the rules, and I try to make sure that my teammates know that it's important to me.

So what can you do within the rules? For one, the crew has to be more aggressive about moving their weight to make up for the fact that the sails are stuck in one position. And when we set up a boat before a race, we decide where we want the unused sails loaded (for example, 60/40 to starboard and slightly aft of middle). Finally, every time there is a sail change, we talk about where the old sail gets stowed so at least it's helping out with boat speed.

Learning from Your Mistakes

I have a theory about learning from your mistakes. It is that when practicing, it's actually good if something goes wrong (within reason) because that means it's not going to happen on race day. If there's a weak fitting on the boat or a flaw in the teamwork or communication, what better time to have it become apparent than during practice, when it's not costing you valuable places in a race? This is yet another reason to push your boat and crew in practice—to expose those weak links and to make those mistakes.

But regardless of whether it happens during the race or not, as long as a mistake or an error happens only *once*, that's really all you can ask. That's what learning is all about. None of us is perfect, and all of us are human. And while you hate to have bad things happen during a race, mistakes do happen, and you recover from them as best as you can. On any size boat it is really important at the end of the day to gather together as a team and to discuss what you learned that day. Doing so both puts a period on the day's events so the team can move forward, and ensures that everyone has a chance to contribute their ideas on how to make things better next time.

During the 2003 *Stars & Stripes* America's Cup campaign, Dennis Conner had instilled in us, the crew, the feeling that we didn't have much time. We really had to make every minute count. So at the end of every training day, I would ask Kenny Read, our helmsman, or Vince Brun, our main trimmer, "What did you learn today?" And I really wanted to hear from them what they learned. Mistakes are a very fertile environment for learning, and that's what we're all out there doing. That's why we race—to get better and to improve ourselves.

～⌒⌒⌒

Marshmallows and Avoiding the Hex

On the starting line it is important to know your competition and to be able to quickly recognize who's who by their sail number or some other little detail of the boat. One of the tricks of the trade is to start near a lesser competitor who's not going to push you hard as you launch off the starting line. In a crowded, big-fleet starting situation, not everyone is going to have a clear lane—and soon more than half the fleet will be a boat length or two behind the leaders. So if you can get a good jump off the line—if you can blast out into that first 30 percent of the fleet—all of a sudden you're sailing against a much smaller group of boats, because 70 percent of the fleet have fallen into the bad air and the wakes of all the boats coming off the starting line so close together. A disadvantage of only a few inches at the start can turn into boat lengths very quickly. You want to be in that top group, and your life is going to be a lot harder when you have the class champion starting right next to you instead of the class "marshmallow."

I can remember when I was first getting into one-design racing. I was racing down in Florida in the 470 class Midwinter championships. We were not doing very well in the regatta, but the one thing I was happy about was our starts. Why? Because the same guy—the class champion—always seemed to be starting right next to me. So I knew I had chosen the correct part of the starting line, even if I was not the fastest boat out there and was soon dropping back. It wasn't until I heard this guy giving a lecture later that year that I realized the error in my assumption. He told the group, "One of the keys that I do when I'm starting is I always try to start next to a marshmallow."

All of a sudden it dawned on me—*bing!*—I'm a marshmallow.

Normally, I like minimizing risk, so I avoid starting near the ends of the line because they usually are more crowded and therefore present a higher risk. But there are times when you've got to go for it, such as when one end of the line is very favored and that same side of the course is highly favored. If the wind is such that it is imperative you go left on the first leg and the pin is highly favored, you have to have a bit more gumption and taste for risk-taking than everybody else. You have to claim your position and have your timing right. You'll sometimes see the top sailors win the pin end in a high-risk start and make it look almost too easy. The reason is that they have put the hex on most of their competition. Nobody wants to start next to Jud Smith in the Etchells or next to Ben Ainslie in the Finn Class. So when they see Ben, and he's really making it clear he wants to start right *here*, more often than not they'll let Ben start right *there*. And sometimes these great guys get incredibly open starts at one end of the line in what should be a crowded starting-line situation.

As an up-and-coming sailor, you can't let the psych factor get to you. Sure—in the prestart you might try to avoid the class champion and start next to a marshmallow, but when it comes to how you approach the boat-for-boat tactics on the open course, nobody gets a break. You treat everybody exactly the same.

Embracing Change

The best sailors embrace change because that is when decisions have to be made quickly and opportunities arise. If you watch a one-design fleet of boats racing in moderate conditions, all the boats go at about the same speed and—except for the guys with bad starts or equipment or crew problems—they all get to the top mark at about the same time. But when the conditions get trickier, the space between the first boat and the last boat increases. This is because there's more opportunity to make a right or a wrong decision in every wave, in every wind shift, and in every change of condition.

Every time a condition changes—be it wind speed, wave size, current, or wind direction—there's always one best reaction on board the boat, and many potential responses that, in varying degrees, aren't as good. If you're sailing upwind on port tack and there's a wind shift to the right, for example, you either tack on it or you bear away in the header and continue on, but you can't keep going the exact same way you're going. You need to make an adjustment. Down the road you will be able to look back and assess whether it was the correct response. At the very moment you make the decision, however, you don't yet have all the information to know what the right move is. But experienced sailors will have a better hunch as to what to do, and they don't wallow.

You can't afford to overthink decisions—especially when conditions are changing quickly. Chuck Robinson, a former Nike board member and the founder and president of CBTF Co. and M Ship Co., once told me, "There's a tendency to overanalyze and overcalculate—to try to get everything before making a decision. When I joined the board of the management consulting firm Arthur D. Little, and attended the first board meeting, I was told that its greatest asset was that twelve hundred employees had doctoral degrees. At that time, the company was making about three or four million dollars a year in profit. And I said, 'You know, there's something very strange to me about this. You have twelve hundred people who have their doctorates and you're making three or four million dollars a year in profit. My company makes *fifty to one hundred* million dollars a year in profit, and I don't have one doctorate in my entire organization!' My point was that you can have all the intellectual horsepower in the world, but if you don't direct it with imagination and willingness to take chances and be creative, it doesn't add up to much."

Any time conditions change, it's a bit disconcerting. The boat gets out of the groove, everything's out of whack, the boat's not going as fast, and you have to make some changes. The sailors who recognize that a change of condition is a great opportunity for gains react quicker and get a jump on the competition. Embrace the change!

I remember a college nationals that we sailed in Chicago. The wind was coming off the shoreline and it was shifty. My crew, Susan Daly, and I were in a two-person dinghy, and the 10-to-20-degree wind shifts were coming every minute and a half. We started in the middle of the line and with every wind shift we either tacked or didn't tack, but we always made a quick decision and stuck with it. By the top mark we were in the lead. It was almost an out-of-body experience. The shifts were happening faster than I could logically think about them, and I was just reacting to them and it seemed like we were doing everything right. Susan and I were fully in the zone. When I reflect back on my sailing career, that was one of my favorite moments on the water.

Hurricane Sailing Sea Story

The closest I've been to dying on a boat occurred pretty early in my career, just before I went off to college at Yale. It was in the fall and we were delivering *Rhapsody*, a 39-foot racing boat, from Connecticut down to Florida for some races. We had completed the first leg of the delivery—from Connecticut to Norfolk—in one long weekend with a full crew of seven sailors. We went back home for a few weeks, then flew back to Norfolk to complete the second leg of the delivery— from Norfolk to Fort Lauderdale. This time there were only three of us on the boat, which, for a 39-foot boat, is shorthanded.

It's not dangerous to sail long distances shorthanded, but everything has to be done more methodically and more carefully—you can't push the boat as hard.

If I ever were to do something like this now, I would check the weather forecast before even deciding to set sail. There's so much information easily available now that planning ocean passages to avoid dangerous conditions is much easier than it was back then. And this particular boat was not really equipped for ocean sailing. We had only a portable shortwave radio on which we could obtain some marginally useful ocean weather forecasts.

It was a warm, sunny day; there were no signs of an approaching storm and, after a nice passage through the beautiful inland waterway from Norfolk to Morehead City, North Carolina, we headed out into the Atlantic for the final leg to Florida.

I was seventeen at the time, and the skipper, Tyler Keys, was a few years older than I. My friend Andy King was the other member of our crew. Tyler may have checked the forecast, but I can't remember ever doing so. I was young and fearless and we were heading to the ocean. Fort Lauderdale was the next port of call, and—in between—adventure awaited.

We were about a day and a half out of Morehead City—a hundred or more miles off the Carolina coast—and the wind started to pick up. Before we knew what happened, we were hit by a "clear" storm—with no clouds—packing hurricane-force winds. At 60 knots and building, the cups on the wind instruments at the top of the mast blew off. And it kept getting windier and windier.

The waves were huge—20 to 30 feet high—giant, foamy breakers. We had too much sail up—the mast was in danger of breaking. So first we wrestled the mainsail down to the deck and secured it on the boom. Next, we decided we had to shift headsails to the smallest sail on board, the storm jib. I can remember struggling up onto the foredeck with Tyler to do the sail change and the waves were crashing and washing over the boat. At times we were waist-deep in water. We had our life harnesses on and we were tethered to the boat as we moved forward—we would almost get to the bow, but then a wave would hit us and we'd be washed backward, sliding all the way until our life harness tether came taut.

Somehow we got the old sail down and packed away into its sail bag and hoisted the storm jib—it probably took us nearly an hour on the foredeck to complete what is normally a pretty simple operation.

I can still remember being up there on the bow at the height of the storm in the middle of the ocean with the giant waves washing over me. All of a sudden, James Taylor's version of Carol King's "You've Got a Friend" popped into my head. I'm thinking, "Wow, what a weird song to be thinking about." To this day, every time I hear that song it takes me right there onto the deck of the boat in the middle of that storm—fighting for my life to stay on board the boat.

We made it through the roughest part of the storm and it slowly dissipated. Every inch below deck on *Rhapsody* was soaked and we were battered, but it was a great experience. As the weather warmed and the breeze dropped, the feeling of accomplishment grew.

The first lesson I learned through this experience was to trust and rely on your boat. Boats are amazing things. Not only do they float, but if you handle them correctly they can perform in conditions that you can barely hang on in. By shifting to the smallest sail, *Rhapsody* survived the storm intact.

The second lesson I learned was to trust in your teammates. I relied on Tyler. If it wasn't for Tyler and Andy on the boat—and all of us working together—there is no way we would have survived. It was almost like we were climbing to the top of a mountain. We moved slowly forward, step by step, until we reached our goal.

Clear Air and Clean Lanes

When you're racing in a big fleet, one of the most important tactical challenges is setting your boat in a position where you can sail in clear air for a long period—a clean lane. It's therefore very important to have a good idea of how wind flows around a boat. On my last two America's Cup teams, we spent a lot of time studying computer animations that help us picture where the disturbed air is relative to the enemy boat. I've heard stories that the *Alinghi* team used smoke bombs on the bow of their boat to show where the disturbed air—the blanketing zone—is coming from. And it's amazing how bent from the true wind direction the sail's exhaust can be. This turbulent air has lost momentum as it has been turned by the sail of the enemy boat, and it therefore has reduced driving power for your own boat.

The general rule is this: the wind hitting your sails is coming from the direction that you feel the breeze coming from—that is, the *apparent* wind flowing on the sails. This is not the "true wind" (the wind direction that a flag on an anchored boat would display). So a telltale yarn tied to the rigging or a masthead wind vane will point in the direction that you want to have clear and open so that you have 100 percent wind power. On a race course in a big-fleet race, of course, there are times when finding a clean-air lane is difficult. If you're in the front of the fleet going upwind, it's pretty easy—anywhere has clean air. But if you've had a bad start or you're back in the pack a little bit after missing a wind shift or two, the lanes close down. So the ability to find a spot where you can sail in clear air going toward your desired side of the course is very important. You don't want to be tacked upon and, therefore, have to do two extra tacks to escape bad air before you can get rolling again. One trick you can use on a windward leg is to set up on the windward "hip" of your competitor. Let's say you're sailing along on port tack, and a starboard tacker is crossing you closely but you want to go to the left, too. You go just past his line far enough so you won't feel any bad air from his sails, and then tack from port to starboard. The goal is to tack so soon—so "thin" on the starboard tacker's windward hip—that he acts as a blocker for you. Any other poor tackers ahead of you who might think about tacking in a lane that would block your clear wind are obstructed from doing that by your blocker. It's a fine line. If you tack too soon, you risk falling into his bad air. If you tack too late, his effectiveness as a blocker is negated.

Going downwind, the trailing boat has the advantage unless you're sailing faster than the true wind speed, like the multihulls that reappeared on the America's Cup scene in 2010. At those speeds, the leading boat gives bad air to the trailing boat even when sailing downwind. But in slower monohull boats, when sailing downwind the leading boats are the ones that have to look for clean air. The tactical challenge becomes balancing out your intent to sail on a particular side of the course for favorable wind, while staying clear of the dense clumps bad air caused by boats behind you that can block your wind. It's hard in a big fleet. Like upwind sailing, you generally try to set up in a lane so you will have the cleanest air for the longest amount of time. Jibes are costly.

When a boat does get on your wind, whether you are sailing upwind or downwind, you have to make a decision: do we stay or do we go, and if we want to stay, how long can we hang in here in the bad air? This is one of the hardest judgment calls in sailing. In general, if you're within about six mast lengths—about eight boat lengths—of the enemy boat, the bad air from their sail plan will adversely hurt you if they are lined up perfectly to hit your breeze. Beyond eight boat lengths you can often live for a long period getting almost full power from the wind.

When in doubt, bail out. People tend to stay too long in bad air. By the time they tack or jibe away, they've already paid too much.

One of the tricks I learned when I first started sailing with Dennis Conner and Tom Whidden on America's Cup boats in a match-racing format is to use bad air to gain. Sound crazy? Well, here's how. If you're behind and your competitor tacks on you, don't tack away immediately. Instead, wait a few seconds until the bad air from the enemy boat actually travels downwind and begins to hit your sails. Depending on the wind speed and how far behind you are, that would mean several seconds to even a dozen seconds before you start to feel the disturbed air. During this waiting period, Tom and DC would keep going straight because their boat's wind was still clear even though a boat had tacked on their apparent wind line. And then when they felt that the disturbed air was about to hit their boat, they would call for the tack. Tacking like this through the bad air means less wind speed, less adverse force, and less wind resistance. By the time the tack is complete, your wind is clear again, So this tack is not as costly as it would be in clean air. If your opponent keeps coming over to tack on you, you can actually gain by tacking through his bad air!

Coaching

Today, with the growth of high school sailing, a lot of good young sailors are benefitting from the advice and support of a team coach who is present not only at practice, but also at regattas. But I see a lot of "soccer parents" at junior races overcoach their kids when they should just let them enjoy the fun of sailing. I come from a self-coaching background. Sure, I had some great instructors during my summertime junior sailing program days, but at the regattas, they were nowhere near as active as today's youth coaches are. In college, on the Yale Sailing Team, we prided ourselves on being one of the top national college teams in the country, and unlike a lot of our competitors, we didn't have a coach. The main benefit of self-coaching is that you are responsible for your own learning. You have to want it, and that type of desire and effort is an important element in success. As for our competitors, their coaches were the ones running the show, taking responsibility for organizing team meetings, practices, and travel. We felt that we were getting better performance out of ourselves and learning more by taking our own leadership and running our own program.

In the last America's Cup campaign I did with BMW Oracle Racing, we also went without a coach, but for different philosophical reasons. There we had eighteen crew on each sailboat, and extra sailors, sail designers, and boat designers riding around in chase boats close behind us, watching our every move. So really we had a plethora of coaches out there; they just didn't have that title. At the end of the day, when we had our sailing team meeting to review the day's activity, there; was plenty of input from guys who were both on and off the boat. So we decided that we really didn't need to hire a coach to simply be one more set of eyes. There were already plenty of different perspectives to go around.

But times have changed, and today the Yale team has a coach, and I fully supported that big change to the team. In fact, all the top college and top Olympic sailing programs operate with a coach. I think the primary reason for this shift is that the science of coaching itself has changed. Where the old-school coach was more of a take-leadership-and-tell-the-competitors-what-they-saw person, today's coaches take more of a creative role of aiding the self-discovery of the sailors.

There's huge value in having a set of eyes off the boat and an outside perspective that still respects the idea that it's the sailors who are the ultimate deciders of what's right and wrong. But to have somebody who can stimulate the sailor's thought processes and inspire deeper exploration of techniques and skills can be extremely valuable for any sailor.

The great sailing coaches of today are really like another crew member on the boat. They don't place themselves above the competitors. And even if you are not doing an Olympic campaign or vying for the College National Championship, there's great value in having somebody from time to time watch you sail and share his observations.

But I still think that the coaching scene is a bit overdone in some parts of the country at the junior sailing level. It's a fine line, because coaches can help performance. But unless they are skilled, they can also contribute to burnout that will ultimately turn the kid away from our sport. The desire to stick with the sport through the high school and college years has to come from within.

～⌒⌒～

What's in My Seabag

The general rule for packing for any sailing trip, whether it be a day sail with friends or a race across the ocean, is to try to pack as little as you really need. This is true for a few reasons. First, all that extra stuff is just extra weight on a race boat— and that will just slow you down. Second, you'll find that some crew members may be watching the oncoming gear, and you don't want to be the person with the biggest bag (unless you have made a lot of cookies or brownies that you intend to share with the crew). And third, good storage places where the gear is guaranteed to stay dry are at a premium on any boat. At the same time, you don't want to be cold, you don't want to be wet, and you want to be safe. You might even want to have your teddy bear with you when you bunk down. But this is not normally a time when you'll have three different outfits to choose from.

Here are some guidelines for what you'll want in your seabag for a race on a big keelboat in moderately temperate climes. For an overnight race, you'll bring one undershirt/T-shirt, maybe two shirts for a ten-day race, and one pair of underwear—two pairs of socks would be extravagant. A nice, fuzzy midlayer jacket or pullover is your best friend when it gets cold out as well as a warm hat and waterproof outer socks. It's very akin to climbers going up Everest. They don't bring another down parka for when it gets 40 degrees colder. They bring an extra layer that they also can use as a pillow.

Whatever you bring, make sure it stays dry. It's heartbreaking to go down below to grab that nice, warm jacket in your bag only to find it soaking wet from bilge water. So ask the owner or the skipper where a good place is to stow your gear, especially if your cell phone's involved. Almost any place on a boat can get wet, and some boats are more prepared for that than others. So it's a good idea to bring a small waterproof bag, whether it be a simple Ziploc bag or a fancy waterproof bag, for any electronics you brought with you. For an ocean race when seabags get tossed around as people move from bunk to bunk, it's a really good idea to have a waterproof seabag, also known as a dry bag. You can get one at almost any marine store.

For a day race, I'll try to bring nothing more than the clothes I'm wearing and my foul-weather gear, which I might keep in a backpack. If you must bring some extra gear, stow it in a high place so it's clear of any water sloshing in the bilge. Or stow it in a compartment that has no access to the bilge, where water could wash from one side to the other.

As far as actual sailing clothing goes, there's nothing more comfortable than a cotton shirt and shorts. But if that attire doesn't fit the weather forecast, you can rug up with some layers. Outdoor clothing specialty companies like Patagonia, REI, and Kathmandu make nice, fuzzy mid-layers, polyester long underwear, and thermal socks. For outerwear/foul weather gear, Henri-Lloyd, Musto, Gill, Atlantis, Slam, and Gul make good, dependable gear. If you're going to be getting wet, make sure you have comfortable foul-weather gear that will keep you dry.

No matter what kind of sail you're on, there are a number of basics to bring with you. Make sure you've got a knife, sunscreen, sunglasses, and a hat. Sun protection is a big thing regardless of how windy and wet it is. I make sure I have one more layer of clothing than I think I'll need. So if I'm going to go out sailing in San Diego Bay on a sunny day and it's 70 degrees onshore, I'll wear sailing sandals, a T-shirt, and shorts. But I also bring with me a nice, windbreaker-type jacket that is water-resistant if not waterproof, or a soft-pile midlayer jacket, and I'll tell my friends to do the same thing. And although everyone on the boat needn't risk their cell phones in the marine environment, it's wise to have at least one on board for safety. It should be stored in a waterproof bag. And I would never go on an overnight sail without my tiny iPod Shuffle and my Etymotic ER6i earphones to help tune out the action on deck and get me in the mood for catching some valuable z's.

✺✺✺

Keeping It Cool On Board

I'm a very calm person on a boat. And when I'm in charge, I try to bring a level of calmness and clarity to high-pressure situations. But I'm not unemotional by any means, and I do not try to hide my feelings. I won't stand up and cheer in the middle of the race, but if we make a good move and get a jump on the competition I will share my delight with the team in a mellow kind of way because first and foremost I'm a team player.

It's like someone making a slam dunk in a basketball game. After a player sinks the shot, you'll see his teammates give high fives all around, and then they get right back and play some defense. In my experience, emotion is a great motivator, and—as long as a leader can channel it in a positive way—it is an extremely powerful force that can lead to great success.

I've definitely mellowed with age. I'm just as competitive, but I'm not as excitable. When I was younger, I could get good and distracted about some really inconsequential detail that wasn't right on the boat. Today I'm much more focused on the big picture, and a lot of noise and drama on the boat doesn't help.

I can play the game any way that works for the team. But if I'm in charge, I try to lead by example, staying calm and cool unless the situation really requires some animation. That's just what works for me. The bigger the boat, the more people on board, and that can result in some pretty chaotic moments during the heat of battle. Since I've done so much big-boat racing lately, maybe that explains why I've gravitated toward this more serene style of sailing.

KISS

As I was coming of age in the sport of sailboat racing while I was in college at Yale, my knowledge and understanding of the incredible complexity of the sport grew immensely. I started becoming aware of the finer points of boat speed and the intricacies of tactics and really applying some of the science I was learning at school into my sailing. For example, my college roommate Stan Honey and I put together a mathematical proof, analyzing from two reference frames the effect of current on a racing sailboat. (To this day I use this proof when somebody is confused by the myth of the lee bow effect.) We were definitely diving very deeply into the sport of sailing from a lot of different angles.

But when it came to actually getting out on the water and racing, it was clear to me that there are some very basic general rules you must honor. While some of my competitors got sidetracked in the intricacies of the pursuit of boat speed, I took a step back. I realized that focusing on the basics—keeping it simple—is where 95 percent of racing success comes from. And I still believe that today.

During the summers of my junior and senior years, I traveled around the country teaching seminars on racing at different sailing clubs. I was amazed to find out during these summer seminars just how complicated people can make their sailing. Granted, it *is* complicated, and that's one of the beauties of the sport of racing—there's always more to learn. But people can get bogged down in the minutiae and not see the big picture, which boils down to just three simple things: having a boat that's well prepared, getting off the starting line fast, and sailing quickly in the right direction.

You may be the kind of person who wants to overanalyze things and make your sailing more complicated than it needs to be. But these basics are the very first rules of success. And until you're at the postgraduate level of the sport, you should definitely put aside all that complex stuff and leave it onshore. Let it seep into your sailing slowly, by osmosis. On the race course, keep it simple.

Getting Kids into Sailing

One of the coolest things about the sport of sailing is that you can keep enjoying it for virtually your entire life. Maintaining the sport of sailing's health requires drawing a broad base of participation from all ages. That means getting young people into the sport and retaining them as they become teenagers and have other forces pulling at them. One of sailing's great strengths is its social side, and that should be maximized. Friends can sail together, girls and guys are equally adept on a boat, and there is also an important cross-generational aspect. I learned so much from the generation before me, and I feel a strong responsibility to try to pass that information on to the next generations.

There are a lot of ways that kids can get into sailing, but they're not going to stay in it unless they're having fun. That often means being involved in an organized sailing program where they have friends and they get to have fun together. There's that social aspect again. It's not just about performance in competition. I see some "soccer-style" parents sending their kids off to international regattas at a really young age, and I believe that's maybe pushing things a little bit too hard. Sailing is not like soccer or baseball or football or a lot of the other sports that kids do only at a young age, or if they really excel at it, they take it through high school and college. Then the career is over. Sailing is something they can keep enjoying and improving their skills in throughout their lives—as long as they don't burn out when they are young.

I think the healthiest junior sailing programs are the ones with opportunities for the adults and the kids to do some sailing together—there is not total age segregation. I was lucky in that the junior sailing boat during my formative years was the Lightning—the same boat that was raced competitively by adults in my home waters of western Long Island Sound. So on the weekends, the top juniors would be crewing for and racing against their parents and the adults from the club, which helped keep the sport healthy.

That unfortunately rarely happens anymore. Nowadays the kids usually sail much more high-performance boats, and the adults tend to sail slower keelboats. While the kids are having a lot of fun out on the water zipping around, they lose the benefit of that cross-generational activity that really helped me and my peers improve our racing. And ultimately this separation of generations by boat type hurts the sport's ability to keep kids hooked. That's just one idea based on my experience. There are lots of ways to try keep the sport healthy and as sailors, all of us have a responsibility for making sailing as attractive as possible for kids coming in and then keeping them involved.

• • • • • • • • • • • IN THEIR OWN WORDS • • • • • • • • • • •
John Bertrand

John Bertrand skippered Australia II *to victory in the 1983 America's Cup, ending 132 years of American supremacy in the competition and earning Bertrand a spot in the hearts of every Australian. Bertrand won the bronze medal in the Finn class at the 1976 Summer Olympics in Canada. He still races in his home waters of Melbourne, Australia, and recently won the Etchells Class World Championships.*

The America's Cup is the longest-running sporting event in modern sporting history, 160-odd years. It started off before the U.S. Civil War and before the modern-day Olympics. And it's intriguing in many ways. From my perspective the Cup is very much people-orientated. Having competed in five America's Cups, my experience is that invariably teams aren't defeated from the outside, they're defeated from within. Even if they're competitive on the water with good technology, they often fail internally. Why? Because of the huge amount of pressure that comes onto these teams. So the question is: How do you build a team—a world-class team—that actually can withstand the enormous pressure, in some cases self-induced, so the organization doesn't collapse?

There's a really interesting book written by Edward de Bono, *Six Thinking Hats*. It's all about the great industrial and engineering breakthroughs we've seen over the past couple of centuries, such as the Trans-Siberian Railway and some of the great innovations in engineering in the early days of the United States. These leaps forward didn't come from large groups of people. Instead, they came from small groups of four or five—maximum six—people. And what de Bono presents in his book, which was a great influence to me in the formation of my America's Cup teams, is that you really need to put together a group of people who have complementary skill sets. So, for example, you need creative people, but you also need finishers. Creative people such as the great Tom Schnackenberg will have a whole series of ideas, and if one out of the ten ideas is great, then it could be a breakthrough, but you've still got to make it happen. So you need people who can conceive of the opportunity and those who will bring it to fruition. And interestingly, you need a negative person to keep a cap on the whole thing; otherwise you'll be heading out into the ozone, where nothing ever gets done. And you need a chairman-type person who's really a facilitator, bringing the various talented people together. So you need people with a mixture of skill sets all working together on the team.

The thing that was a breakthrough for me was to understand that everyone doesn't need to be the same as I am. In fact, that's not a good deal. You need people with separate talents who can be complementary. So when we analyze successful teams that are really robust under extreme pressure, it becomes clear that they are comprised of people with different yet complementary skill sets. It's very complex to put together the ultimate team that can win the America's Cup. But assuming that team has a strong technology base, if they get it right, they are very difficult to kill off, and historically we've seen that. I think we've seen that with the

Alinghi team; certainly in the early days they were very, very tough, and it was very hard to beat them.

The America's Cup provides a really interesting study of team-building at the ultimate level. Taking a closer look at where team meltdowns occur, I believe they are typically caused by a lack of compatibility, a lack of a sense of really strong values such as trust and integrity. The strength of the team is not so much when everything's going right, it's when your backs are to the wall. And it is important to have fun regardless of the environment you're working in—even when the pressure is enormous. That's the real strength of a winning team; that's when the rubber hits the road. In an America's Cup team that's crumbling, often the first sign can be seen in the partners of the sailors; if they are booking air flights home, things have gone bad.

You absolutely need world-champion-level people to be part of these teams. But I've never met a world champion who's a normal person. You've got to be screwed up in some way to get out of bed at all different times of the day to do extraordinary things. That's not a normal, relaxed person. You're dealing with extreme personalities, and that's also part of the challenge of putting together these world-class teams that must be truly robust under extreme conditions.

In the Cup, you're talking about big groups of people working over a long period of time. Most athletic endeavors are much shorter. Today, we're talking about three-to-four-year buildups. And there's this push of getting world-class talent on board early, but with them comes all their strong egos and idiosyncrasies. The trick is finding that ultimate mix of people and incorporating a set of values that will make this team absolutely, literally indestructible. Because in an event such as the America's Cup, you can't practice the stress of that final eleventh hour— when, after years of preparation and months of elimination rounds, you head out on the starting line for the first race of the Cup Finals. The pressure is enormous, the world's press descends on these teams, and it's a new domain for many of these people. You need an indestructible group to survive and thrive in that arena.

This Is Supposed to Be Fun

Maybe the most valuable lesson I've ever been taught about sailing came during the fall semester of my sophomore year at college. My crew, Susan Daly and I, were doing well in team practices, consistently at the top of the fleet, but at regattas we seemed to be just a bit flat. We were putting in the time, practicing hard and doing what seemed like everything necessary to be successful on the college circuit. But we never seemed to be able to put it all together at the big regattas—we always fell short. It got to the point that I was really getting stressed about our performance because I felt we *should* be doing so much better.

Then one night after team practice, Olympic medalist Glen Foster (bronze medal, Tempest Class, 1972 Olympics) came up to give an after-dinner talk to the team. As I was listening to his entertaining story about his experiences at the Kiel Olympiad, something inside of me clicked. He wasn't talking about the special light-air jib with the fuller head that he and his sailmaker developed and unveiled at the Games; he wasn't talking about his conservative starting technique or his crew's heavy-air spinnaker-pumping technique. He was talking about how much fun it was to be in the Olympics, the competitor friends with whom he shared a laugh on the dock before racing, and the thrill of representing his country. He was talking about *enjoying* his sailing and all that is a part of the sport.

For me, it was an epiphany, and it slowly sunk into my thick skull.

At that particular time, I wasn't having any fun with my sailing. The fact that I was now representing my university and sailing on the varsity team, along with the higher expectations and my own competitive ego, all built up until I was just taking my sailing too darn seriously. I wasn't smelling the roses anymore, or enjoying the beauty and fun aspects of the sport that had drawn me to it in the first place. The next day in practice, I shared my thoughts with Susan on the boat before the racing started. Susan listened to this confession of my sins—of my treating sailing like a grim professional—and it was music to her ears. As it turned out, Susan had been putting up with my ever-increasing stress level and didn't like it one bit. The less fun *I* had sailing, the less fun she had sailing with *me*. I promised her that I was going to make a real effort to have more fun with our sailing, and to enjoy the privileges we had in being able to spend time on the water and race for Yale.

Almost overnight our performance jumped. We started really clicking at the regattas, and our results rocketed. It was no small coincidence that our Yale team won the College Dinghy Nationals that spring. Looking back through the perspective of several decades of America's Cups and countless high-pressure events, I still consider that moment when Glen Foster unknowingly unveiled that important lesson to me to be a watershed moment in my career.

Choosing the Right Sail

On bigger keelboats, you often have a choice of what jib to put up, and generally the choice is dependent on wind speed. For example, a boat with a two-headsail inventory carries a smaller, heavier sail and a bigger, lighter sail. In the J/24 class, which was enjoying its heyday as a racing class during my twenties, there is a choice between a large genoa jib, which is employed in light wind, and a smaller, nonoverlapping jib, made out of heavier cloth that is faster when the wind is smoking. But the hard part is deciding which sail to use when the conditions are right on the edge of each sail's range—crossover conditions. It's an important call because your pick can decide the race.

When the J/24 class first came out, the boat was set up with a double-grooved headfoil with the intent that crews could perform a jib change during an upwind leg. Although this sort of headsail shift is routinely done on bigger boats, it's not a fast maneuver on a smaller keelboat because several crew members are required to stop hiking out and move to the foredeck to help pull the new sail up and wrestle the old sail back on board. On a J/24-size boat, it's simply not worth the cost of the sail change on a short-buoy-race-length windward leg. So within a few years, the headfoils were removed by the top boats in the class in lieu of a simple jib hank system on the bare-wire headstay. The switch made the boats simpler to sail and removed the option to make that jib change in the middle of an upwind leg.

Back to sail selection. I've learned that when you're wavering, the decision of which sail to choose should be based on two factors: average wind speed and sea state. The general rule is "Set up for the lulls." So if the wind is really puffy—with short periods where you are out of range with the genoa, but longer periods of lighter winds—then that would sway you toward the bigger genoa, because the cost of having the genoa up out of range is less than the loss that the smaller jib would suffer in the lulls. As for sea state, if you're sailing in smooth water—such as in an offshore wind situation—you can carry that big sail up to a higher wind speed because accurate steering is possible. In the smooth water, you can sail your boat on that fine line slightly closer to the wind so the boat doesn't overheel and still keep the extra area and horsepower of the big sail. By this precise "pinching" you might end up sailing a touch slower, but much closer to the wind than with a jib, and the net VMG (the speed made good toward the wind) is a winner.

However, if it's rough, with the waves "bigger" than the strong wind, and you're getting big waves building up with the big breeze, then you have to go to that small jib sooner. This is because the boat *is* getting pushed around more by the waves, and you simply can't steer as accurately—your angle of attack to the wind is varying by 5 degrees or more every time a wave throws the boat off course. If you had the big genoa up, every time the boat got pushed away from the wind, the sails would have a higher angle of attack and the boat would over-heel and slide sideways. So in those conditions go with the smaller jib and sail at a slightly faster boat speed (and lower course) than you would with the bigger sail. It may seem counterintuitive that you sail faster through the water with a smaller sail than with the big sail, but I've seen that again and again—not just in a class such as the J/24, where you have two jibs, but also in the bigger ocean racing boats, where you have multiple headsails to choose from. Because of the different performance characteristics of different sails, I always consider changing the target boat speed after a sail change.

Three Essential Knots

When I was thirteen years old my family moved from Ohio to coastal Connecticut and I started sailing in a junior sailing program at Norwalk Yacht Club. I was about three years behind my peers, so when I was learning to sail they were already several steps ahead of me. Maybe for that reason, I became really good at using ropes and tying knots. When I was fifteen, by tying my knots a little faster than the rest, I won the Marlinspike Seamanship Trophy in a competition against juniors from yacht clubs all over western Long Island Sound. I love ropes, I love tying knots, and I particularly love trick knots. But there are just a few knots you've got to have in your repertoire if you're going to be a sailor.

Bowline This is my favorite knot to tie, and there are a bunch of different ways to tie it. Its use is ubiquitous on a sailboat, as it can be used to attach the control ropes to any corner of any sail.

Two round turns with two half hitches This is another very, very useful knot. Getting those two turns wrapped around something reduces the force on the bitter end, allowing you to tie the hitches without fear of the rope pulling out of your hands. A word of warning: don't use this knot on something that shakes or moves quickly, as it can become untied, whereas a bowline hangs in there better for those applications. So the round turns and half hitches are better for a temporary knot (because you can tie it when the rope is under load) or for a line that will be under a steady, static load.

The cleat Wrapping a rope on a cleat is a must-have skill for any boater. I learned a long time ago that on sheets and lines that you adjust frequently, you don't apply the locking hitch that you see in a lot of knot books. But on a line that remains fixed in place—such as a halyard—you do apply the locking hitch. The key in either case is applying one full wrap around the base of the T-cleat before you do your figure eight so that the load from the rope is absorbed at the base of the cleat and the figure-eight part is not being pulled so hard.

The key characteristic of any good sailing knot is that it is easily untied even after being subjected to extreme load. The bowline is a star in this department because you can simply "break the back" of the knot and it comes loose. There are plenty of knots that will work doing the securing part of the job, but only a few that can be untied without the aid of a pair of pliers or a knife.

Copy the Experts

To the nonsailor, two identical boats should logically sail at the same speed, given equal crews and the same wind and wave conditions. But when you get deeper into the sport, you realize that just small changes in "identical" equipment can make all the difference on the race course in terms of raw speed, pointing ability, and even ease of handling. And this fine-tuning often comes from changes you make to your boat, rig, or sails *before* you leave the dock. For example, a few turns on the headstay adjuster will change the mast rake. Coupling that with an adjustment in the position of the bottom of the mast at the step can result in a boat with a much different balance and feel when sailing.

When you really get down to it, the combinations of tuning variations available on even a simple boat are essentially limitless. And every little change—every twist of a rigging turnbuckle, every adjustment in the tension of a sail control—is either better or worse for a particular condition. But being able to ascertain the effect of these changes, and quickly appreciate if the tuning change is better or worse, is incredibly difficult. Sailing faster than the competition requires finding the right blend of tuning for *all* the controls, not just the primary ones (mainsheet and jib sheet) that are constantly adjusted on any race boat. So how do you get the perfect tuning for the perfect condition?

Copy the experts.

In one-design classes, most top sailmakers will have a tuning guide available to help you get your mast set up with a proper rigging tension, fore and aft rake, prebend, etc. If you're getting into a new class, or just want to get up to speed with the competition quickly (which certainly sounds good to me), follow this tuning guide and/or talk to the top sailors in your fleet and copy what they do. Once you're at that established baseline, you can then make your own experimental tweaks to see if you can gain even more performance. But at least your boat will be at a good starting point, in the same ballpark as the top competition.

Quantifying the effect of small tuning changes is hard to do out on the water even in the most controlled testing environment. At best, the results of a change are usually not apparent until many minutes after the adjustment is made because of the variables in wind between boats. Believe me, it's not easy to be able to confirm that a small change is better or worse. I've been on an America's Cup team where it takes more than a week of controlled testing to start seeing definitive results of a single small change.

It's easy to make the wrong conclusion, too. You might do better in a race after making an adjustment, but that could very well be because you got lucky and got a wind shift in your favor. So you might attribute your success to the tuning changes when it was actually the wind shift that won you the race. There are so many variables in a race that being able to ascertain which adjustment and which element had what effect on the race is very, very hard to do. But getting up to speed quickly by copying the top guys in your class is a sure thing that will give you an easy jump on much of the competition.

〜〜〜

My Gurus

Over the years, I have had the good fortune to sail with some amazingly talented sailors. Here's a list of some of the sailors who have had a significant effect on my life and sailing career.

Ted Jones   In the late 1960s, Ted was an editor of what is now *Sailing World* magazine. When my family moved from Cincinnati,

Ohio, to Rowayton, Connecticut, we wound up living across the street from his family, which included three sons, who became my good friends. Ted was a good sailor in both small and big boats, and through the magazine and his books, he had an important journalistic voice in the sport of sailing. Thanks to Ted's efforts, I got into the Norwalk Yacht Club Junior Sailing Program my first summer in our new town. He bent the rules so a nonmember's child could participate in the junior racing program. I never looked back. Not only did Ted get me into sailing, he also had a study filled with sailing books and magazines that I just devoured. Without his influence, I probably never would have gotten hooked on sailing.

Tom Whidden   Today Tom is the president and CEO of North Sails, the world's largest racing sail manufacturer. But back when I first met Tom, he was working for Sobstad Sailmakers, a small local sail loft in eastern Connecticut, and he was running the racing program for a local 42-foot race boat in Long Island Sound owned by Dick Hokin by the name of *Love Machine*. Tom was a great dinghy sailor. He sailed Finn dinghies and other small boats, but he was starting to make his name in big-boat sailing. I had the good fortune in my early college years to sail with Tom and the *Love Machine* crew right before Dennis Conner picked him to be at first a sail trimmer, and ultimately Dennis's right-hand man and America's Cup tactician. Tom taught me a lot and gave me a lot of opportunity to build my confidence racing at a very high level on *Love Machine* when I was still quite young.

Dick Wilson   Kendrick Wilson Jr. was chairman of Avco Corporation. His son Jimmy was in the Junior Sailing Program with me at Norwalk Yacht Club, and he had a beautiful 45-foot racing boat called *Troon*, named after the famous golf course in Scotland. Dick (or "Mr. Wilson" to his young crew) decided to invite Jimmy and a bunch of his junior sailing peers (including me) to be part of this racing crew. *Troon* was one of the largest racing boats on western Long Island Sound at the time—and most of our competition were sailed by all-adult crews. Dick gave us a real vote of confidence and a unique opportunity by bringing us aboard. So at a very young age, I got to learn some of the big-boat skills that most of my peers didn't get until they were much older, because big-boat programs usually aren't opened up to younger kids.

Steve Benjamin and Stan Honey   Steve, Stan, and I were roommates at Yale, and together we headed up the Yale Corinthian Yacht Club (YCYC) for three of our four years. We met as kindred spirits when we were freshmen and realized that not only did we love sailing, but also we saw the Yale Sailing Center, which was ten miles outside of New Haven, as a great place that we could call home. So we made a pact that for each of the next three years we were in college, one of us would be commodore of the YCYC. This is because the commodore got to choose which undergraduates lived at the sailing center. We pulled it off by showing more interest and being more involved in the club and in the maintenance of the boats and equipment than any other student. So we had a corner on the market and lived at this amazing sailing center for the next three years (and probably for another year or two after graduation). It took them a while to kick us out. During our tenure on the sailing team, we won several national championships, including the coveted Dinghy Championship (with teammate Dave Perry co-skippering with Steve in A Division). In different years, both Steve and I were awarded the most prestigious award in college sailing—the Intercollegiate Sailor of the Year Award. Steve went on to win an Olympic silver medal in the '84 Olympics and is one of the top sailmakers and racing sailors in the world today. His attention to detail and quest for a speed edge are legendary, and by example he taught me about sailing fast. Stan went on to win innumerable offshore races, including numerous Transpacs, and the around-the-world Volvo Ocean Race. He has set lots of records, including the fastest nonstop sailing time around the planet on the trimaran *Groupama 3*. Both Stan's scientific approach and his love of navigation made a big impact on me. Back at Yale, we were sailing 420s, Lasers, 470s, and 505s, and talking about our sailing dreams. I think each of us sort of egged one another on, and supported our dreams to go farther in the sport. It's fun to see the guys I was racing with back in college still being leaders in the sport of sailing today. And Steve and Stan definitely are.

Dennis Conner and Paul Elvström   In my teenage years, I was most influenced by the famous Olympic sailor from Denmark Paul Elvström. Paul did what no one had ever done before, dominating Olympic sailing by winning gold medals in four different Olympiads. I pored over all his books on tactics and technique, and his message "Always have fun with your racing" really resonated with me. I got a chance to meet him when we invited him to Yale for a regatta several years after his final Olympic campaign (crewing for his daughter in the Tornado catamaran class; they finished just out of the medals).

At the other end of the spectrum is Dennis Conner, Mr. America's Cup. When I was younger, I respected people who had cut their teeth in dinghy sailing—big-boat sailing for me wasn't where it was at. The people who had learned to sail in small boats and then were applying these skills—whether in other small-boat racing such as the Olympics or in larger boats—were the ones I looked up to. I felt that small-boat sailors had an edge because the feedback and the sensitivity and the skills you learn on a small boat are not possible to learn on the much heavier "duller instrument" of a big keelboat. But slowly I was lured into that world of big-boat sailing, too. Thanks to my friend Tom Whidden, I got invited to sail with Dennis, first in a few offshore races before finally teaming up with him to win my two America's Cups (Dennis's third and fourth!). His leadership and motivational skills, attention to detail, focus, desire, and ambition are second to none. I've learned a lot from DC thanks to being on the same boat for many years in a lot of different races.

∽∽∽

Finding the Edge

The classic line about designing and building an America's Cup boat is that because weight has such an effect on performance, the boat should be built so lightly—so on the edge—that when it crosses the finish line in the final race, it breaks in half and sinks. And in 1995 and again in 2003, America's Cup boats did sink or break in half, but unfortunately, neither of them occurred after they crossed the finish line victorious. So finding that edge is something that for builders and designers at the America's Cup level is very important, but obviously very risky.

When you think about it, there are some classes and class rules that don't allow you to build a boat that's going to get anywhere near breaking apart in the kind of conditions you would ever possibly encounter in a race. But there are others, such as the America's Cup, where the construction requirements are less strict, and the designers and builders and engineers push the limit. Why? Well, in the case of the America's Cup boats that competed from 1992 until 2007—the International America's Cup Class—every pound that could be saved anywhere on the boat could then be "spent" in the bulb of lead at the bottom of the keel fin, four meters below the water. Moving that weight down to the bulb results in extra horsepower, extra righting moment, that provides a powerful fulcrum against the forces of the wind. So, especially in this class of boat, there was a high incentive to shave as much as weight as possible in the hull and deck equipment.

But ensuring that the boat doesn't break in half too early requires having an intimate knowledge of your boat and the loads to which it will be subjected. This requires a good scientific knowledge of the materials used in construction and of the forces on a boat. At the America's Cup level, teams put sensors on their boats to get a feel for what the actual loads are. Then a new part can be designed with an acceptable margin of safety. I don't think any designer and builder in his right mind would ever agree to build a boat that's right on the edge. It's not good public relations when your boat sinks. It comes down to a question of how much margin you put in there. And the more knowledge you have of where that fine line is—whether it's in a structure, or whether it's in your crew—the better your engineering decisions will be. That's where experience, time on the water, knowing your equipment, knowing the materials, and having better computer tools really pay off.

In normal racing, where the boats aren't engineered and built to the edge, you still want to sail the boat to the edge. Consider the example of sailing downwind in medium wind on a Laser dinghy. When sailing downwind, the boat will naturally start to rock back and forth laterally. If you don't do anything to stop it, it will, like a pendulum, rock and rock and rock—each swing a little bigger than the last—until boom, the mast hits the water, and you've capsized. However, it's amazing how fast you're going right before you capsize—that's the fastest moment. So keen one-design sailors spend hours out on the water even in the light airs simply finding out how far they can push the boat in a variety of different maneuvers and when sailing downwind, on the edge of capsizing. There's no way to be able to sail like that without practicing. And when you do capsize, you've got to get back in the boat and do it again. And again, practice in this case really *does* make perfect.

• • • • • • • • • • • **RACER'S RULES** • • • • • • • • • •

John Thomson

John Thomson, chairman of Thomson Industries, Inc., of Port Washington, New York, is one of the most successful amateur helmsmen in the world of yacht racing. From the mid-1980s into the mid-2000s, John owned a series of 40-to-50-foot racing sailboats (all named Infinity) and amassed an enviable record, including a first overall at the 1996 Kenwood Cup, besting a fleet of professional helmsmen. Here are John Thomson's racing rules:

1. Attitude is what's really important.
2. Listen a lot.
3. Teamwork.
4. Try to involve people.
5. Flexibility.
6. Doing nothing is a strategy.
7. Have the patience to wait.
8. Slow down and gain.
9. Never, ever give up.

• •

~~~

Weather Signs

Although I majored in meteorology at Yale, I am always learning something new about the weather. When you're sailing, the weather is of paramount importance—it can be your best friend or your worst enemy. It still amazes me how a perfectly delightful day on the water can turn into "men against the sea"—and back again—in just a few hours' time.

A good portion of my pre-race preparation in any boat, for a long or a short race, is studying the available weather information. Even for just a weekend buoy-racing event I'll spend at least half an hour the morning of the race on the computer studying the various forecasts and getting a feel for the conditions and the dynamics of what will be driving the day's weather. Although today's technology allows you to get an amazing amount of weather information from the Internet—no matter whether you are sailing within cell phone distance of the shore, or thousands of miles at sea—I still believe that every sailor should be in close touch with his environment and be able to read the signs in the sky that foretell what kind of weather is headed your way. Here are some tried-and-true classics that reward sailors who keep their eyes open. They can be surprisingly accurate:

- Red sky at night, sailors' delight. Red sky at morning, sailors take warning.
- Dew on the decks, wind from the sea. No dew on decks, wind from the land.
- When the wind speed exceeds the temperature, head for home.
- When smoke descends, good weather ends.
- Seagull, seagull, sit on sand; it's a sign of rain at hand.
- The higher the clouds, the finer the weather.
- Rainbow to windward means rain is on the way. Rainbow to leeward means rain has passed you by.
- Mackerel sky, twenty-four hours dry.
- When the clouds/sky cover change, expect a wind change.
- The wind will come from the clearest direction on the horizon.

Living the Dream

There you are. You're in the gym at six-thirty in the morning, you haven't had a day off in three weeks, and you're about to go out on the water and do the same thing you've done for the past three weeks—spend every available daylight hour straight-line, two-boat testing with an America's Cup team. Your team-mate leans over and says, "This is it; this is as good as it gets."

You're living the dream. And you realize that there are thousands of sailors who would give anything to be where you are, on the best America's Cup team. And yet, the grass is always greener, and from the inside looking out, it's a lot of long hours, drudgery, and repetition. But it's all part of the preparation that's necessary at the America's Cup level, and if you aren't willing to live the dream, there's always somebody else who is.

Steering in Waves

When you're going against them, waves will slow the boat down. But when you're going with them, waves can speed the boat up. When racing, waves are opportunity. They change all the time, so therefore with practice, skill, and good technique you can use them to make gains against your competition. Sailors who are used to sailing in smooth water and face waves for the first time usually suffer from the encounter. Here are some of the techniques I employ when dealing with waves.

Probably the most common waves we face on the race course are wind waves—six inches to two feet high—a short chop that builds up with an afternoon breeze. My friend Bill Gladstone, who runs the North U. education program, has a colorful description of the steering technique employed in these sorts of waves. He says that when sailing to windward, you want to try to "crush" these obstacles. Because the boat slows every time it smacks into a wave face, you need to apply a little bit more power. But because the waves are so close together, you really can't steer or adjust your course for every wave. Instead, you add power by steering the boat slightly broader to the wind—maybe ease the sails a little bit and sail at a little faster speed and wider sail angle than you would in the same wind conditions in smooth water.

At some point the short chop gets bigger and the wave lengths get long enough that you can address individual waves and benefit. Always remember that every time you steer the boat with the rudder, you're slowing the boat—the rudder is a brake. But in this case, the speed loss from turning the rudder is less than the gain in having the boat approach each big wave at the most efficient angle possible. As the wavelength gets longer and those two-foot waves get far enough apart where you can actually steer around them, it's just like when you're paddling a surfboard out through the surf line in the ocean. You don't ever want to put a surfboard sideways to the waves. With all that surface area presented to the wave it will be pushed very hard, and loss of control and a long swim back toward the beach to retrieve your board is the usual result. Instead, if you try to point the board exactly perpendicular to the oncoming wave, the bow of the board (or in our case, the bow of the boat) will present the least possible surface area and resistance to the energy of the wave, which is going the direction opposite of where you want to go. The result is that the wave passes by without a huge push backward.

As a general rule, when the waves get bigger and their wavelength grows farther apart, when sailing to windward, steer the boat up toward the oncoming wave. We're not talking about a 20-degree course alteration; it might be just 3 degrees.

And as the bow goes over the top, slowly bear off and sail a slightly wider sail angle as you come down the wave. As the waves grow in size, don't steer around every single wave, just the larger ones. The smaller ones aren't worth the speed loss from using the rudder for steering and also the loss from the sail power as you pinch up. It's a technique that you learn—up the front of the wave, down the back of the wave. In a dinghy or a small keelboat, when you reach the top of the wave and you begin to bear away, it helps to hike out extra hard for a brief moment, because the sails are temporarily farther up in the atmosphere where the wind is stronger.

The third type of wave we might encounter is the long-period ocean swell. In San Diego we have classic ocean-swell conditions on many days. These big waves are created by winds hundreds of miles away. For this reason, you can experience significant swells even in very light winds. Their wavelength is very long, and the height of the wave can be quite big. Even on a light-wind day in San Diego, you could experience a six-foot swell going through with crests that are more than a hundred feet apart. In this condition, when sailing to windward one of the worst possible things you can do is try to steer around the waves. They're just too far apart, and there's not enough wind to be able to accelerate easily to make all of the steering worthwhile. One of the biggest mistakes lake sailors make when they come to San Diego is to trim the sails too tightly and try to point too close to the wind. So one of the tricks you learn in light-air ocean-swell conditions when sailing to windward is to free up the sails— ease them out, and try to steer as little as possible. Instead of trying to steer and correct for all that pushing around that the swells do, you just pick an average course, have the sails slightly eased out, and rumble through it. Sometimes the sails will be luffing and sometimes they will be overtrimmed as the boat is thrown up and down by the swells, and you might be able to counteract some of that with jib and mainsheet movement, but keep the tiller rock-steady.

Sailing downwind, waves can be a great help. If the waves and wind are big enough, it's a piece of cake to catch the boost from a wave and surf along with it for some period of time. Lighter, more modern keelboats can really get up and go in these conditions, riding the same wave for impressive gains. Multihulls and fast dinghies can even sail faster than the waves if the wind is right.

Downwind, the tricky bit is in the marginal conditions, when you can almost but not quite catch the waves. Pumping the sails at just the right time (sort of like a surfer paddling at the right moment to catch a wave) and even making a hard turn to point the bow downhill—perpendicular to the wave—can help initiate a surf in a keelboat. But these actions all come at a cost. Remember—turning the rudder always robs the boat of speed. And any time you pump your sails, you are taking them temporarily out of their optimum aerodynamic position in the wind. So if the pump does not provide the boost needed to catch the wave, it, too, will cost boat speed. In general, I'm a fan of trying to sail the boat more smoothly in these marginal conditions. Years ago I learned a tip that I still remind myself of when sailing keelboats in marginal surfing conditions: keep the bow pointed downhill.

How you deal with waves very much depends on the type of boat you're in and the kind of waves you're facing. There are gains to be made, but you have to first identify which sort of technique will work to your advantage.

My Five Favorite Places to Sail

Honestly, it is impossible for me to be definitive about this list of my five favorite places to sail—I've had some great days sailing in so many places. Literally anywhere your boat will float could be the next addition to your list. But here goes:

Hawaii   Anytime the water temperature is less than the wind speed, you're in real trouble, but when the water temperature is over 80 degrees Fahrenheit, and the wind speed averages more than 20 knots, you don't get any better conditions than that. Almost any kind of boat is plain old fun to sail in windy, warm weather, so whether you're on a sailboard or a big old keelboat, Hawaii is number one on my list. It's also beautiful approaching the islands from the mainland. I've done a number of races to Hawaii from the mainland, and you can see the Big Island peeking out over the clouds more than a day before you finish. And the wind tends to funnel and pick up in the channels between the islands—it's like the race is building to a natural crescendo. You start to see more dolphins and seabirds, and I swear you can smell the flowers. It's a magical island chain to have as a destination. You feel like you really have achieved something when you sail to Hawaii. Maybe that's how Captain Cook felt.

Skaneateles Lake   One of the Finger Lakes in upstate New York, I first visited Skaneateles when I was just two years old, and I've been there almost every summer since. The water is fresh and drinkable. It's a big enough lake that you can get some good breeze and, if it's windy enough, some steady winds—for a lake. It's just a beautiful, beautiful place to sail. The lake also has historical significance in the sport of sailing. Hull number one of Olin Stephens's famous one-design class—the Lightning—was built in Skaneateles. They also used to have a large Star class fleet. Today the powerboats greatly outnumber the sailboats, but there are still a couple of sailing clubs on the lake that occasionally hold races.

Western Australia   This favorite of mine is on the coast of Western Australia, specifically Fremantle, where I won my first America's Cup sailing with Dennis Conner and the *Stars &*

Stripes team. I have such fond memories of that win, and on top of that, it's just a great place to sail. The coast off of Fremantle is protected from the big ocean swells by a series of barrier islands. In the summer months they get an incredibly strong sea breeze, which they call the Fremantle Doctor. The Doctor comes in at more than 20 knots most summer days and cools off the coastline—taking it from being a very, very hot desert-like climate to close to the temperature of the water, which is in the low 70s. You can't go wrong with a good breeze and sailing out along the coast or up the beautiful Swan River.

The Swedish archipelago   The waters around Stockholm are a pretty magical place to sail. Not only are there a seemingly end-less array of islands with narrow and wide waterways and incredibly picturesque Maine-like rock coastlines, but in the summer months there are twenty hours of sunlight. There are almost no hours of true darkness, and dusk lasts quite a long time. There's something really special about exploring the coastline anywhere near the Arctic Circle, and seeing people who are trying to pack twelve months of outdoor time into just a couple months.

Anyplace new   The list of places that I get to go to as a pro-fessional sailor is incredible. Places such as Newport, Rhode Island; Southern California; San Francisco Bay; Sardinia, Italy; Cowes, England; Auckland; and the Caribbean seem to be on my regular circuit, and all of these are great spots to sail. But for me part of the fun of the sport is going to new places and exploring them on the water. Recent additions to my ports of call include Cape Town, Salvador, Brazil, and La Maddalena, Italy. I enjoy the experience of sailing someplace new, whether it's learning the tactics and figuring out the tricky local knowl-edge that you have to learn anytime you race anywhere, or just getting that unique perspective that you do looking in from the water of the local community and geography. It's all good.

Pimp Your Boat

Recently, I've been spoiled because I've been sailing with America's Cup teams and big-boat racing programs that want for nothing. The owners want the best boat they can get, so they hire the best designer(s) they can, and they build the mast and the hull out of the best materials they can get their hands on. And they have a maintenance program that ensures the boat is sailing with the best gear available. I guess I've paid my dues enough to have earned my spot on these cutting-edge campaigns. But earlier in my career, things weren't always so cushy.

I've sailed on plenty of boats that have been put away wet and have a "to do" list as long as their mast. Most of the sailboat racing in the world is done by people who play the game recreationally. Make no mistake about it: they want to win the weekend race just as much as Larry Ellison wants to win the America's Cup. But these are "regular" boats, often used as much for cruising and recreation as they are on the race course. This is not the America's Cup arms race, where the "perfect" race boat is the ideal. But still, these weekend warriors can take a page from the grand prix level of racers by considering upgrades to their existing equipment.

Far and away, the most important areas to concentrate on are the sails and the spars. Assuming your boat is structurally strong, it's not going to break, and the bottom is smooth, your first priority should be to have a fresh suit of sails—designed and built by the top sailmaker for that class of boat. If I was getting into a one-design class, I'd copy and get some sails just like ones the top guys in the class are using. I wouldn't try to go out and design my own sails or find a local sailmaker and have him working with me to develop something secret. I'd just buy whatever sails the guy who won last season used. It's amazing what a fresh suit of sails will do for performance—they certainly are the engine of the boat.

If you look at the grand prix level of the sport, it's the same thing. America's Cup teams focus on their sail inventory (including their solid wing sails), and design and build many, many sails—hoping to come up with the fastest designs. They do this for a reason: because of the importance of the sail in the overall speed package. However, you can't forget your mast—it's the next most important item on my upgrade list. You don't have to go out and buy a new mast, but you've got to make sure it's well detailed and tuned well in both the fore and aft plane (rake and prebend) and the athwartships plane (side tuning). If you are sailing a one-design class, check with your sailmaker to ensure that your mast is equivalent to the model being used by the top sailors in the class.

Next on the potential upgrade list would be the running rigging. With all the high-tech fibers available in rope, there is no need to have any control line on the boat thicker (and heavier) than necessary for easy handling. Focus first on upgrading the primary control lines—the spinnaker sheets, the jib sheets, and the mainsheet—before spending money on the lesser-used lines. As for the deck equipment, there's always newer and greater stuff available (sort of like cell phones), but usually an upgrade is not worth the cost and has little effect on performance. If you do want to play with your deck layout and equipment, focus first on weight savings, then on ease of use and reducing friction.

The key is setting reasonable priorities. If you have a limited budget, aim your hard-earned dollars at areas where you get the biggest bang in performance. I see too many racers wasting time and money on upgrades that simply won't affect performance anywhere near as much as a good day on the water practicing with the full crew!

~~~

Tragedy Hits Home*

In 33 years of ocean racing, neither of us had experienced a man-overboard situation of this magnitude: on Friday, May 24, 2002, soon after the start of the Block Island Race aboard the 66-foot *Blue Yankee*, our bowman Jamie Boeckel, 34, was lost at sea as a result of being injured and knocked overboard when the spinnaker pole broke during a sail change. After hours of searching, we were unable to recover his body, but the events of that night will stay with us forever, as will the lessons we drew in its aftermath. Jamie's memory is best served if we can help prevent future catastrophes.

Before leaving the dock in Stamford, Conn., *Blue Yankee*'s owner Bob Towse held an in-depth, thoughtful meeting covering safety and strategy. We discussed our man-overboard procedure, the need to wear lifejackets (we were all wearing them at the start), the location of safety equipment (a list was posted), and communication procedures. Although safety harnesses were available, no member of the crew felt the relatively mild conditions (offshore winds and smooth seas) warranted putting one on. Following this pre-race session we headed to the race course.

Blue Yankee won the start and set a fast pace. Just after sunset, 25 miles from the start, the wind increased from 12 to 18 knots, triggering a call to change from the Code 3 asymmetric spinnaker to the Code 5 asymmetric. As the new spinnaker was hoisted, the wind built dramatically. Standing at the bow, Jamie struggled to release the shackle holding the tack of the old spinnaker. Something was preventing the shackle from opening, and as seconds passed, an unseen gust caused the boat to round up.

This article, which I wrote with Gary Jobson, first appeared in the August 21, 2002, issue of Sailing World *magazine, and is reprinted with the permission of the authors and* Sailing World, *all rights reserved.*

Both spinnakers luffed violently, the spinnaker pole broke, and it hit Jamie hard. He immediately went into the water.

As Jamie slid past the leeward rail, crewman Brock Callen (who'd been at the mast hoisting the spinnaker) saw that he was floating face down, unconscious. The boat was sailing at 13 knots, and Brock made a split-second decision and dove in. Neither he nor Jamie was wearing lifejackets.

Brock reached Jamie in seconds and tried unsuccessfully to revive him. Meanwhile the crew launched the man-overboard package on the transom and worked feverishly to douse the two spinnakers as the broken pole slashed across the foredeck and the wind built to 35 knots. We then started the engine and tacked toward the blinking man-overboard light, returning in about six or eight minutes. As we did so, we alerted the U.S. Coast Guard on the VHF.

After a brief search, we found Brock near the man-overboard gear, but Jamie was missing. The water temperature was 53 degrees, and Brock was near hypothermic shock when he was pulled aboard. He told us he'd held Jamie afloat for a few minutes, but that Jamie was unresponsive and eventually he'd been unable to keep Jamie from sinking.

Five boats retired from the race to assist us when they heard our call on channel 16. At least 15 other boats also came to our aid. We were still in Long Island Sound, not far from Bridgeport, Conn., and the Coast Guard and local police arrived within 15 minutes of our call. We were impressed by the quick response, which included a helicopter to help with the search.

At midnight, Connecticut Department of Environmental Protection officers led by Sergeant Jim Wolfe boarded *Blue Yankee*. They were businesslike yet cordial while taking statements and surveying the scene. Just before departing Sergeant Wolfe said, "From what I can tell, you guys did everything you could—especially Brock—I'd have him as a shipmate any time. I hope this incident won't discourage any of you from racing in the future." It was a soothing comment at a time when we were feeling considerable anguish.

It was eerie returning to *Blue Yankee*'s berth in Stamford near dawn with one crew missing. A few words were spoken, and we went home.

Sailing can be hazardous, so we have a responsibility to prepare our crews, our boats, and ourselves to react swiftly and efficiently during an emergency. A live situation is always tougher than the theory, but preparation can make a critical difference. In the weeks that have passed, we've developed a list of thoughts and recommended procedures for ourselves and others in similar situations. We encourage all sailors to think through, in advance, what you would do.

1. Make sure the crew understands how to launch the lifesaving/man-overboard gear quickly, and where all safety gear (lifejackets, radios, etc.) is located.
2. Make sure the entire crew understands the man-overboard procedures (e.g., shout "man overboard," spot the victim, jettison lifesaving gear, etc). Pre-assign positions in case of an emergency.
3. When performing a difficult sail change, such as a spinnaker peel, bear away enough that broaching is not a concern—especially if "locking off" a spinnaker sheet to free up a primary winch.
4. Wear your life jacket anytime you like and certainly on deck at night or other times conditions warrant. Expand the window of what you consider to be "life jacket" conditions and spread that attitude. If your life jacket is uncomfortable, get one you'll wear—even if that means choosing a float coat, vest, or other non-Coast Guard–approved device.
5. At night, carry a pocket strobe or at least a waterproof flashlight.
6. Have a big knife in a sheath readily accessible in the middle of the boat, as well as a personal knife.

7. Have a working GPS on deck with an easy-to-operate man-overboard button.

8. If a man-overboard occurs, release the man-overboard gear immediately. Spot the victim, and if they appear to be in trouble, have someone grab extra flotation and jump in with them. This advice runs counter to conventional wisdom and many man-overboard "manuals," but if the victim is really in trouble, extreme measures are in order. Of course, if the boat is short handed or conditions are too difficult, then weigh the possibility of losing a second crewmember against the boat's ability to return promptly.

   • Do all you can to keep the victim in sight; assign one crew member this duty. At night, the man-overboard gear should have a light, making returning easier.

   • Get the boat turned around as fast and effectively as possible. Usually that means dropping headsails, but not always. It may mean cutting away sails, but not always. Each situation is different and requires a cool assessment of the big picture. The worst thing you can do is panic. For example, after dropping headsails, the crew of *Blue Yankee* took an extra few seconds to ensure all ropes were out of the water before engaging the engine. Wrapping a line in the propeller would incapacitate the engine and severely limit the boat's ability to return in strong winds.

   • When problems occur, immediately make an emergency call on VHF channel 16. In a race, other boats will be nearby.

9. Any time you hear a call for help on the VHF or see a dangerous situation, stop and assist. Everyone on the water has a responsibility to themselves and each other.

10. During sail changes and maneuvers the most experienced sailors (watch captain, skipper) should watch the evolution carefully and calmly point out solutions to problems as they occur.

11. Maneuvers should be discussed in advance, particularly the course to steer and a plan if something goes wrong.

12. Treat every day on the water as if it were special—really special—because it is.

Blue Yankee had a talented crew. The boat was well prepared and was sailed in a normal way. The crew performed well in a tough situation, but we do have lingering questions: What if Jamie had kept on the lifejacket he wore at the start? What if we could've predicted a rapid, near tripling of the wind speed? (In daylight we'd have seen the gust coming, eased the spinnaker sheet before locking it off, and borne away further to minimize heel and risk of broaching.) What if we had changed spinnakers earlier or been able to release the snap shackle faster? Could we have cut away the spinnakers and returned sooner?

This sad event deserves on-going study with a look at both gear and procedures.

Leave Your Ego on Shore

I've had a very diverse career in sailing. I've founded two America's Cup teams. I've skippered on the Pro Match Racing Tour. I've navigated two America's Cup winners. I've been tactician on grand prix boats. And at this point in my career, I still do a lot of sailing in a variety of different positions. At one regatta I may be navigator and number three or number four in command on a boat, and the next week I could be the guy in charge. And the week after that I might be just helping out on a friend's boat.

To be honest, I enjoy it all. To me the sport of sailing isn't about one person—no matter how talented he or she may be— it's about the *team*. I enjoy the variation of sailing in different positions, and the challenges and the mental and physical processes that are different about each of those positions. It keeps me fresh and it keeps me learning. I understand that the boat isn't as good as me alone; the boat is as good as *everybody* on the boat. To me the most magical time in a competitive environment is when you're sailing with a great bunch of people who aren't caught up in where they stack up in the boat's command hierarchy, but who all work together as a team and are on one page. They're all making decisions and they're all contributing in their assigned slot on the boat.

I've sailed thousands of miles with guys who can steer the boat better than I can, who never get their hand on the wheel in a particular race. That's just the way the crew is divided that particular day—it's not the way it will always be in life. Once you realize that the next race offers a new chance for you to excel in your role on the boat and help make your team as good as it can be, the better off you will be.

Boat-Handling Perfection

In racing, straight-line speed is important, but so, too, are the maneuvers you make each time you change course. Even though the boat slows down when it's turned, every maneuver—every tack, every jibe, every mark rounding—is an opportunity to gain distance on the competition if you perform it efficiently (or lose distance if you don't). The key to making the most of every maneuver is simply breaking it down and analyzing it bit by bit.

So just like a kid who learns a complex piano part right-hand first and then left-hand second, a team should go out in light air to develop their light-air tacking technique, in moderate air to develop their moderate-air tacking technique, and in windy conditions to develop their heavy-air tacking technique. This is because the optimum technique for each maneuver will vary depending on wind speed. You've got to get these moves so ingrained within you and your team that even in the highest-pressure moment you could possibly imagine, you'll do the right thing. That's why practice is important and why teams that want to leave nothing on the table add boat-handling to their list of things they work on.

There's also a certain level of pride that comes from being a good boat handler. You're not afraid to go in and battle in a tight situation—say, at a mark rounding—and this gives the skipper and the crew confidence to push into tight spots when the tactics and the strategy make sense to do so. Along with the good boat-handling that comes from practice comes the confidence to really fight for a prime spot on the starting line, or to make a tight turn inside a pack of boats at the leeward mark. Even if you don't have the biggest budget or the best equipment in your fleet, if you're the best boat handler out there, I guarantee you're going to feel good about your racing and turn some heads.

The bottom line in any maneuver is to lose as little speed as possible. Depending on the maneuver, it may include significant lateral body movement of the crew to help turn the boat (and minimize the use of the rudder, which causes drag) and to accelerate it on the new course, as in a roll tack. Or it may involve analyzing and reworking the timing of the sequence of steps in a team maneuver, such as an A-sail jibe on a larger keelboat.

Consider the Great Dane, Paul Elvström, who revolutionized the sport of dinghy sailing and won a gold medal in four consecutive Olympiads (1948–1960). His boat-handling was one of his greatest strengths. He trained so he could hike out harder and longer than his competition. His mastery of many of the kinetic techniques such as roll tacking and pumping the mainsail downwind was decades ahead of anyone else. Today when you watch a group of high school or college sailors aggressively work their dinghies in masterful rolling maneuvers around the course, you are seeing the fruits of the seeds that Elvström planted decades ago.

✍✍✍

Do Your Homework

The great sailors make it look easy. They may be naturally talented in the sport of sailing—both athletically and mentally—but I can guarantee that it doesn't come that easy. Behind every great sailor is an awful lot of time spent practicing the basics back at home—putting in the long hours in the cold of the spring and fall off-season—honing the skills they need to win on the racecourse.

The same applies for all of us trying to improve. There's no fast track to winning. It takes practice. It takes preparation. It takes working out the routines. Over and over again. Doing your homework by taking the time to practice is a key ingredient in becoming an accomplished sailor.

There are two things I do immediately before any regatta. First, I try to schedule at least one practice day on the day before the first race. I know that after some time off, I sail the boat better the second day than I do the first day—even if it's been just two weeks since I've been on the very same boat. This especially applies when I'm sailing with a new crew. This sail also helps me orient to the local conditions and possibly gives me an idea how the wind may shift on the very next day during the racing. Second, I do my homework on the weather. With the help of the Internet, I can check the forecasts (you should see my list of favorite bookmarks—it's one of the most valuable things I keep on my computer) of what the conditions will be on the next day of sailing, and get a little bit of a leg up on the competition.

Boat Speed Magic

When Team New Zealand won the America's Cup in 1995—going 5–0 in the Cup Finals against Dennis Conner's *Stars & Stripes* team—taking the Cup out of the United States for the second time in America's Cup history, they simply blew away the competition. Their boat—NZL-32, *Black Magic*—was a spectacularly fast IACC boat. And in a match race, Russell Coutts was a good enough starter that he could get off the line at least equal to the competition. From that point, their speed edge was everything.

In all racing, boat speed is important. But when you try to pin down what it is about a particular boat that makes it fast, you'll get a variety of different opinions. In the case of *Black Magic*, the designers might say it's because the hull was narrower than those of the other boats. The sailmakers might disagree, pointing out that the boat had a revolutionarily stiff carbon fiber mast with a new type of diagonal stay system—the "x rig." The appendage designers might point to a more efficient keel fin shape and more powerful low-cg bulb. And the sailors could weigh in with their own opinions, such as saying that the crew trimmed the sails differently. After hearing all the different opinions, you soon start to realize that it's impossible to put your finger on just one thing that makes a boat go fast.

A fast boat is like a winning sports team—a variety of elements all blended together to great effect. A team effort. It's not like *Black Magic* had the fastest rudder, the fastest keel, or the fastest hull. It was a blend of all the components and the way the crew used those tools that ultimately resulted in a superior product: better boat speed around the course. That's why boat speed is such an elusive component to pin down. While you make a list of the components that are important in boat speed—from a good aero package (sails and spars), to a good hydro package (the hull and the underwater components), to a great crew who are strong enough and know how to shift gears in the changing conditions—those doesn't necessarily mean that you'll have a fast boat. It's a blend of all the above—and more—and we are on a never-ending quest to get all those parts working together in the right proportions at the same time.

What keeps everybody guessing and coming back to race is that, in fact, there are parts of the perfect boat spread out across every fleet. And it's the team that has the best overall package and the best boat speed that will win the race. But that doesn't mean they've done everything right.

• • • • • • • • • • • • IN THEIR OWN WORDS • • • • • • • • • • •

Ben Ainslie

Ben Ainslie is a four-time Olympic medalist, gold in 2000, 2004, and 2008 and silver in 1996. He won the World Youth Championships in 1995 and was awarded the title of British Yachtsman of the Year in 1995, 1999, 2000, and 2002. He was elected ISAF World Sailor of the Year in 1998, 2002, and 2008. Recently Ben's been focusing on his big boat and match-racing skills with great success.

Learn to respect and get on with your peers.

As a young, aggressive Laser sailor I would push hard on the water and end up in countless arguments and shouting matches. I was younger than the guys I was racing against, racing in the 1996 Olympic Games at nineteen, and I felt I had to make it clear to the older, more experienced sailors that they couldn't intimidate me.

There was one French sailor in particular who was a problem for me, and for whatever reason we would always be in the same patch of water pushing for mark room or whatever. In a warm-up regatta to the Olympics we were both on the final run to the finish; he was leading and I was second. I was fast downwind and I began reeling him in and was about to pass when he began screaming at me for cheating and breaking rule 42. At this point

the "on-water judge" came up to us both and gave the
Frenchman the penalty for too much rocking. As he was doing his
penalty turn I sailed past and made some sly remark to wind the
guy up, but he lost it, and I mean really lost it. It died down and
all was seemingly forgotten until we began racing in the Olympics
a fortnight later and the same guy protested me in race two. The
protest was a complete fabrication, but I was fortunate that the
TV coverage of the race had picked up the incident and proved
that I was in fact on starboard tack, not port tack, as was being
claimed. The protest was dismissed and I put it behind me as a bit
of bad blood and gamesmanship.

Eight years later we were both sailing in the Finn class for
the 2004 Olympics. Again, in the second race we were both sailing on the extreme left of the first beat with few other boats
around, and I thought I could easily cross the Frenchman. As I
crossed on port tack he pulled his bow away and claimed an
incident even though nothing had happened. We had words; he
then took back his claim and apologized. At the very end of
protest time the Frenchman put in a last-minute protest with no
witnesses. I had no witnesses, either, as we were both on the far
side of the course. Under the rules the onus was on the give-
way boat to prove his innocence, and the jury decided to back
the Frenchman. I was incandescent; as the favorite going into
the Games I had sailed a poor first race and now had to substi-
tute a second place in race two with a disqualification. I was
now twenty-first overall after two of the ten races, and my
Olympic dreams were all but over.

The lesson is that you should always, at least on the outside,
show respect to your peers and try to forge good relationships. In
my case a petty squabble eight years previously very nearly
derailed my Olympic Games in 2004. As you grow older and
move into bigger boats sailing with teams, this is even more
important. You may very well be racing against a guy one week
and then be racing with him the next. As hard as it can be, keep
your aggression on the water and your issues to yourself. You
never know when you might need a friend.

❦❦❦

Shorthanded Sailing

Shorthanded sailing is, by definition, sailing a boat with less than a full crew. When racing, you need a full crew to be able to turn the marks and maneuver the boat swiftly in competition. But even when you're cruising or day sailing—on a boat of any size—having a full-size crew allows you to operate your boat most efficiently.

That said, when we sail recreationally, we often have less than a full crew of experienced hands. And sailing your boat with less than a full entourage is a great training exercise and a good way to learn about your boat and hone your skills. In a way, you're performing shorthanded sailing in overnight racing when the crew is standing a watch system where only half the crew is on deck sailing the boat. Sure, if you need to make a major maneuver then you wake up the off-watch crew to get some extra hands on deck to help out. But if it's not a major maneuver, you let them sleep and everybody just does a bit more work, maybe holding two ropes instead of one and taking a little extra time to execute it.

I can remember the first time I ever took out a 420 dinghy by myself and managed to put up the spinnaker. A 420 is a two-man boat, so putting up a third sail (the spinnaker) when you are singlehanded requires some serious multitasking. On a dinghy, you can't tie off the tiller—you have to use your weight to steer the boat when you let go of the tiller to handle all the lines by shifting your balance laterally. The steps involved in putting up a 420 spinnaker singlehanded must be executed more slowly than double-handed, but as you go through the process, you quickly learn techniques to make the job easier.

Probably the most important technique you learn in short handed sailing is to keep things simple—to avoid really strenuous and difficult activity. Say you're sailing in a race with a full crew, and you want to change the jib. Unless it is blowing a gale, you do it the hard way. You maintain course, drag the new jib up to the foredeck, and grind it up on its halyard. You then drop the old jib, dragging it back on board with your fingernails with the help of several other friends wrestling the sail down with you. Meanwhile, the boat is sailing at nearly full speed, spray is coming over the bow, and you're right on course and losing only maybe 5 percent or 10 percent of your speed with the crew weight off the rail and up on the bow. But there's no way you can do that type of maneuver when shorthanded.

When shorthanded, or with a less experienced crew, you can't stay on course and do a racing jib change. Instead, you learn to reduce the pressure of the wind by turning downwind, blanketing the headsail with the mainsail so the wind is pushing mostly on the mainsail and with not much pressure on the jib. Another added benefit to bearing away and reducing the load is that the boat stands up—it isn't heeling, and nothing is flapping and shaking as it would be if you were still sailing along close-hauled. A broad reach is the easiest point of sail for a lot of reasons—the boat is upright, so it's easier to move around on the deck. If there are any waves, they are passing under the boat less frequently and at a more gentle angle. And the wind speed felt by the sails—the apparent wind—is at an all-time low because the boat's motion is subtracting from the wind. And then with the boat pointed nearly downwind, you drop the old jib and put up the new one, taking your time. Depending on the size of the boat, it takes only one or two people up on the foredeck to pull down the old sail. Then, once the new sail is hoisted and the old jib is bagged up and cleared away from the foredeck, the halyard and sheets can be pretensioned *before* you turn back up to your desired course. Sure, this "easy" way of changing the jib may cost you five minutes compared to the "hard" way when performed by a full crew, but when sailing shorthanded, doing it the hard way would be slower and more dangerous for the entire crew.

Of course, there are races where big boats are raced single-handed or doubled-handed. The whole exercise teaches you lots of seamanship skills, such as turning down and releasing the pressure to help facilitate a sail change or other activity.

When you're trying to improve your sailing skills, pushing your limit by sailing your boat shorthanded is a really good way to learn some of the techniques that will make it easier for you even when you have a full crew. Then if you're taking out friends who don't know how to sail and you don't want to subject them to grinding winches and getting wet up on the foredeck, you'll be ready with these shorthanded techniques that make sailing seem really easy. Your guests will thank you when they return to the dock with their clothes still dry and the skin still on the palms of their hands!

Perfect Practice

My friend Jonathan McKee, who won a gold medal in the 1984 Olympics in the Flying Dutchman class with teammate Carl Buchan, tells a story about how he and Carl hadn't put in as much time practicing as did some of their competition leading up to the Olympic Trials. Carl had a full-time job, and Jonathan was working, too. So they made a pact that every minute they spent out on the water was going to count. Whenever they left the dock to sail out to the starting line at a regatta, that for them was practice time. They didn't just cruise out to the race, they sailed *hard* all the way to the start. They were using whatever time they did have on the water and maximizing it.

Very few of us can say we have enough practice time for most aspects of our day-to-day and professional lives. Where does all that time go? During my "off-season" (from the

America's Cup) racing, I sail a lot of events with teams where practice time is very limited. It's common for the crew to fly in a day or two before the start of the race, giving us only one or two practice days before the regatta begins. So as a bit of motivation, one of the first points I make to a crew at our first team meeting is in the form of this challenge: let's make whatever time we do have for practice really count.

When talking about an America's Cup campaign, Dennis Conner pointed out, "Time is not your friend." There is only so much you can do to prepare before the racing begins. So whatever the amount of time you have carved out for your sailing practice, try to make time your friend by setting realistic goals and using whatever time you *are* on the boat wisely for full-on practice, from the very moment you leave the dock.

Learning from Maritime History

The sport of sailing has a deep tradition. When you look way back to the British Royal Navy and all the rituals and conventions that were involved in seafaring through the years, you realize there were very good reasons for those traditions. While we no longer scrub the decks every morning when we wake up in the middle of a race, as our oceangoing forefathers did, we do scrub the decks and hose off all the salt spray after sailing to avert salt's corrosive effect. It's important for me to understand and learn about the traditions and history of sailing. It gives me a much better perspective on my own place in this great sport to which I have dedicated my life. There's a plethora of great books—fiction and nonfiction—about the early days of sailing. Head over to the library and check them out. You might get hooked!

Conservative Sailing

The pinnacle of college sailing is the Dinghy Nationals, the Henry A. Morss Memorial Trophy. Every team that qualifies enters two crews—an A Division crew and a B Division crew—and they compete in a series of races that decides the national champion. When I sailed this event, thirty races were sailed, fifteen in each division. Consistency counts, as we learned when we studied past Morss Trophy statistics on our way to our first Nationals in Chicago my sophomore year. The winning team's average finish in each race was fifth place.

In collegiate sailing, the boats are rotated—you get to sail in every boat during the course of the regatta—so if there are a few duds in the fleet it all evens out. The courses are short, so it's not just about raw boat speed. Nobody is going to go out there and win every race. Even the best tactical sailors sometimes get a bad start, and on a short course (the races take about twenty minutes each) there isn't enough time for them to claw their way back up to the front by the finish. We quickly realized that the key to winning a Nationals was not to bang off a bunch of risky firsts and seconds, but to really concentrate on sailing conservatively and maximizing our odds. This meant starting in the middle of the fleet, and not hitting one edge or the other edge of the race course too soon. And while this conservative style of sailing is effective even in a shorter series, it really pays off in a long regatta such as the Nationals, where there are so many races and you don't get to discard any of your scores. The concept of keeping it conservative— not going for the risks, and just sailing within yourself—was very, very important, and my Yale team won our first Nationals by using that approach.

Time for a Swim

There we were sailing around the Hawaiian Islands in the Around the State Race, and at the southwestern corner of the Big Island of Hawaii, there was no wind at all. We had been working hard for about an hour and a half trying to eke out any gain from the wind and the waves that we could, but there was nothing to be had. It was smooth water, the sails were hanging limp, there were no cat's-paws, no zephyrs, and it was very, very, very hot. So all the crew jumped in the water—that is except for one guy, a twenty-year-old sailor from San Francisco who was still on the helm, frustrated that the rest of crew had abandoned him. And that guy's name was Paul Cayard. Now if you've followed the sport of sailing, you know that Paul became one of the real superstars of the sport—winning a plethora of races in many different boats including the coveted Star Class World Championships and the around-the-world Volvo Ocean Race. He also steered the losing boat in two America's Cup matches.

Paul probably wanted to jump in the water, too, and he wasn't overtly upset with us for taking a dip, but he kept trying to get the boat moving. You've got to give him credit for never giving up, but in my experience there are times when just taking a break from the racing, rather than just driving yourself nuts, can end up putting you in a better frame of mind to go to battle when the wind does come in. It sure felt good to cool off and go for a swim.

Hyper-Focus

It goes without saying that concentration and focus are important parts of doing any job well. But let's be realistic here—most racers are not full-time sailors. We're all human, and we bring our problems and our egos and all sorts of distractions with us onto the water. When I was in college, we invited Olympic bronze medalist Glen Foster to come and give us a talk. One of the things he said made me realize that it's okay and only human not to be 110 percent focused all the time.

I'm a very intense person on a boat. I don't look at the beautiful sky at night and I don't look at the beautiful waves out on the water—I'm thinking about the race. But other thoughts do come into my mind at times, and I realize it's okay to be human and that there is some limit to the focus. But I also realize that, especially in buoy racing, if we only have the energy to apply our whole focus for short periods of time, then we should try to prioritize when those times are.

Without question, I believe that the last three minutes leading up to the start and the three-minute period right after the starting gun are far and away the most important times in a short-buoy race—at least on average. Why? Because that's when little gains you make can be parlayed into an insurmountable jump on the fleet. Get your bow ahead a couple of inches off of the starting line with a better launch and you keep clear air, and the three boats around you fall back. On a short course you can usually check those three boats off your list; you've already made the fleet against which you are racing that much smaller.

I try to employ this technique of hyper-focusing during points in the race that I see as being important—like the start in a short-course race. I psych myself up and throw a switch and say, "Okay—you know it's all on here. I'm not going to care about what people think of me, I'm not going to care about how good I 'should' be against these guys. I'm not going to think about anything else and get distracted, I'm just going to think clearly, make good decisions, and execute and try to sail as perfectly as I can."

And then at some point off the starting line, there's probably a natural little relaxation that occurs. But getting that total focus and prioritizing the times when it mattered were big steps forward in my sailing.

◦◦◦

Making Your Move at the Turn

In around-the-buoys racing, the goal—once you get off the starting line—is to find clear air and really work on sailing the boat fast and hitting the wind shifts without being impeded by the other boats. But when you get to the turning marks, the entire fleet compresses. This provides a great opportunity for leaving boats behind you, and you should look at every mark as a golden opportunity for you to make a big move forward.

However, doing so requires preparation. You need to set up for the mark rounding based on where the fleet and the wind are so that you have the inside position and the right-of-way coming into the mark. You need to understand the racing rules so well that you're confident of your tactics when your bow is within a few inches of the other boat. You need to have exceptionally good boat-handling so you can keep the spinnaker up to the very last minute before taking it down—gaining a few more inches and maybe a precious overlap that allows you to pass several boats. This preparation begins to takes place about halfway down the leg as you begin setting yourself up for the compression of the fleet in the mark rounding.

And there's another big chunk to be gained on the exit, as you execute the rounding and then escape from the mark. Again, this puts a premium on boat-handling. If the spinnaker is all cleaned up by the time you reach the mark, then the sails can be trimmed smoothly and accurately, crew weight can be in just the right place so the boat is accelerating, and all eyes are focused on what the best escape route is. Do we tack right away? Do we foot off and keep going straight? Where is the cleanest air away from the trailing boats still sailing downwind to the mark?

Mark roundings are a golden opportunity to gain places, but also a point in every race where the risk of loss is significant. Gaining ground at the turns requires preparation, knowledge of the rules, excellent boat-handling, and above all, a real focus by the entire crew.

࿇

Positive Thinking

I think of all the real winners I've sailed with over the years—guys such as Russell Coutts, Dennis Conner, and Ted Turner—and they all share one trait in common: they exude a confidence that makes the crew feel good about where they are. You know these guys have lost as many races as they've won. Yet every time they get out on the water, their confidence resonates throughout the boat. This helps everyone not only stay upbeat—even if things are going poorly in a race—but also feel good about their own participation on the boat. It's trite to say that it's important to have a positive attitude in competition, but it's not always such an easy thing to do.

Only one boat is going to win a race. There are lots of times in every race when you're dealt small adversarial blows. If you have a positive general focus and a good feeling that you and your boat are up to the task, then you can get through these. I think back to my own Olympic campaign in the Soling class where there were regattas where my crew and I just stunk it up. We couldn't buy a wind shift, and our boat speed was awful. But instead of being beaten down and feeling sorry for ourselves, we tried to stay focused on the positives—that we were one of the top U.S. Soling teams, that we individually were champion sailors and knew how to play wind shifts and knew what it took to make a boat go fast. And we focused on the fact that the problems we were having at that particular regatta could and would be dealt with—they weren't insurmountable. They were just part of our Olympic campaign and our quest to be the best we could be.

Staying Warm If Not Dry

One of the things that can wreck a day out on the water quicker than anything else is being cold. I remember when I was a kid, the standard sailing outfit was blue jeans and a sweatshirt. If it was cold, you'd wear a couple of sweatshirts. And when you got wet, you got *really* cold. Then I got my first set of foul-weather gear, which was so stiff and uncomfortable that you could barely move in it, and it seemed like the gear kept the moisture *in*, not *out*. There were some nights on overnight races back then when I was as cold as I've ever been in my life. Nowadays there's no excuse for being that cold on a boat.

On a boat, there are going to be times when you get wet, whether you choose to because it's warm and windy and you're just happy to get the salt spray on your face, or because it's cold but you're working hard and sweating like crazy inside your foul-weather gear. Regardless of how wet you might be and how you got wet, staying warm is all about using layers of the right type of clothing instead of relying on one heavy piece of warm clothing. The idea is to maximize the air space underneath your outer layer—your foul-weather gear in really wet conditions—so there's more air between the different layers.

When it's going to be cold and wet, your innermost layer should be made of material that wicks the moisture away from you, and that means your good old cotton T-shirt has to stay on shore.

You might find the right underlayer at your local boating-supply store or at an online chandlery. But outdoor-sports-oriented stores such as REI are full of high-tech camping clothing that's perfectly suited for layering and made of a variety of synthetic, polyester-type fibers such as Capilene. Synthetics aren't as comfortable against your skin as cotton, but they are getting closer, and since they don't absorb water, they are way better when you're wet, clammy, and cold. One bonus with underlayers made of these high-tech synthetic fibers is that if they get really wet you can simply take them off, wring them out, and put them back on. Your body heat will dry them out. Better to try to keep all your underlayers including your socks dry from the start by judicious use of foul-weather gear.

In offshore racing, you usually have only one shirt and one pair of socks (extra weight will slow you), so protect them from wetness with great care! Speaking of feet, lately, unless it's going to be really cold, I've been leaving my sea boots at home and wearing waterproof socks over my regular thermal socks, and then just putting my sailing sneakers on over the top. Of course, I'm not doing the bow like the good old days, which probably explains some of my attire shift. And don't forget what your mother taught you: a significant percentage of your body heat escapes from your head, so keep it dry and warm.

It's important to be comfortable when you are sailing, so make sure you have the right clothing for the conditions. When it gets really wet and cold, a good set of foul-weather gear and good layering technique are the secrets.

The Best Nautical Joke

I was told this joke years and years ago. It's still the best boating joke I know.

There's a watch captain on a big U.S. aircraft carrier—say, the USS *Enterprise*. The mammoth vessel is steaming along, and the captain sees a light of a ship in the distance. He calls to the ship on the radio: "Ship bearing 300 degrees at latitude 52 degrees 47 minutes north, longitude 113 degrees 14 minutes west, this is the U.S. aircraft carrier *Enterprise* calling you. Please alter your course immediately." No answer. He calls again, "Ship bearing 300 degrees, this is the U.S. aircraft carrier *Enterprise*. You're on a collision course, alter your course immediately."

Again, no response.

So the watch captain calls up the big chief on the intercom, the admiral, who is asleep in his bunk down below. The admiral comes on deck and he's steamed for being awakened. He immediately demands that the watch captain tell him what the problem is. "Sir, there's a ship headed right at us," the watch captain tells him as he points at the radar screen. With his attention now focused on the rapidly closing threat, the admiral gets on the radio: "This is the USS *Enterprise* bearing 120 degrees from you. We're the most powerful naval vessel on the ocean. I demand that you alter course immediately."

All of a sudden, over the radio comes a crackle and a sleepy voice that says, "I don't care *who* you are, mate. This is the lighthouse keeper and *you* better alter your course."

Keep It Rumbling

One of Dennis Conner's favorite sailboat racing axioms is "Boat speed is king." Of course, most short-buoy races these days are run on a windward-leeward course—straight upwind and downwind. And when you're sailing upwind or downwind, it's not all about your raw speed, it's also about the direction in which you're sailing. For example, sailing upwind is a balancing act between the angle at which you sail—how close to the wind you're sailing—and your speed, which naturally increases as you bear away from the wind. The driver's challenge is to find the optimal sailing angle relative to the wind. That is where the boat is making the best VMG or velocity made good to windward (or leeward). But that optimal angle changes with the conditions, so as the breeze changes in velocity and direction, you're constantly shifting gears.

In light wind it's hard to maintain that perfect optimum VMG angle. When sailing upwind, if you get just a tiny bit too thin (too close to the wind), the boat speed just plummets. So in these conditions there's a real value in erring on the faster side of that optimal angle. A fundamental principle that is not obvious to the new sailor is that when the boat is going faster, the underwater foils (keel or centerboard and rudder) will work better and provide more lift. In fact, in light air, you can often end up *netting* a closer-to-the-wind course by bearing off a bit and accelerating. As the keel or centerboard becomes more efficient in the faster water flow, your boat's leeway drops off dramatically so that you will actually end up sailing a closer-to-the-wind course than if you had kept the boat at the slower, closer-to-the-wind initial angle. And, of course, your boat speed will be much faster.

With boat speed also comes maneuverability, which is always helpful. So although bigger keelboats with sailing instruments may have a "target boat speed," there are many times—especially in light air—when the first focus is on getting the speed up. Only then do you worry about pointing up closer to the wind. Many times when I'm sailing along upwind, racing against other boats that seem to be pointing higher than me, I'll repeat this mantra to myself: "Keep it rumbling, just keep it rumbling."

A few years ago, one-design ace and former Sailor of the Year Jud Smith crewed for me in a local Etchells race, and he used those very same words of encouragement. That's because as soon as the boat speed goes down, your VMG toward the wind falls off a cliff. And in light air it takes precious time to reaccelerate a boat with a load of lead in the keel and get it rumbling again.

Also, you should consider your boat's tacking (or jibing) angle when trying to find that perfect groove. For example, in strong winds, some boats sail very narrow angles to the wind. In 18 knots of wind, a 12 Meter tacks through about 70 degrees. Down in Fremantle during my first America's Cup, Dennis Conner really focused on rumbling because if you can gain an extra tenth of a knot of boat speed by bearing off just half a degree, the net VMG gain is huge. Conversely, in light air, when the tacking angle of the boat is over 90 degrees, it takes much more of a speed gain per degree of course alteration to net a better VMG.

In general, when sailing upwind or downwind, the best sailors get the speed first and then worry about sailing at a slightly better angle to the wind. Keep your boat moving. When in doubt, err on a slightly faster speed.

$\sim\!\sim\!\sim$

Haven

In this day and age, with all the distractions of life onshore—cell phones and e-mails and text messages and more—sailing to me is a haven for getting away and turning a laser-sharp focus on a single something. I enjoy the process of race preparation and then getting out on the race course giving it my all. In that sometimes short period, I go from being my normal distracted twenty-first-century self to becoming very focused and committed to one task only: to try to help the boat win and to do the best job I possibly can in my role with the team. You can't go at it half-assed—you really have to turn off your personal life. It's not something I look forward to doing for long, long periods of time, and in fact I think at some point everybody reaches their limit. That's why in the more recent Cup campaigns that I've been a part of, the teams really try to consider the burnout factor and build in breaks and vacations so that the sailors are still as fresh as possible when it's time to go racing. But to be able to concentrate on one task for a short period—like a mental sprint—is both satisfying and quite rewarding. That is, until I open my e-mail box at the end of the race and have to dig through everything!

Digging Deep

One of the attractions of attending Yale was its philosophy of encouraging a broad-based liberal arts education. Yale intended that all undergraduates obtain a balanced education from a variety of different disciplines. They didn't want students just studying science or just studying math. They saw the undergraduate education as one where you should get a broad, liberal arts smattering of a lot of different disciplines.

My science professor from the Geology and Geophysics Department (where I was majoring in meteorology) once took me aside and said, "Peter, you know Yale wants to expose you to this broad background of knowledge, but there's also value and reward in life that comes from diving deep in a particular subject." He drew a horizontal line depicting Earth's surface. And then he drew a wedge with a little arrow going underground, illustrating the information available if you really dig below the surface. I've thought about that many times in life, and I realize that he was absolutely right. There's a reward in having made that extra effort, making that deeper commitment to doing something great. If you're in competition, then by digging deep, you probably will get an edge—at least in that area. You can't do it all the time without risk of losing focus of the big picture of your life. But by focusing deeply on a subject you exercise your brain and your life resources a little bit more than you do on a normal day-to-day basis. No pain, no gain!

Safety

There are two aspects of safety afloat. One is the safety equipment and procedures that you have onboard the boat, and the other is how you operate and run the boat. And of the two, the latter is *way* more important.

Having all the lifejackets, flares, man-overboard gear, and a knife on deck is one thing, but actually operating the boat safely is much more important. I'm not saying you shouldn't have all the required safety equipment—they're helpful—but how you move around on the boat, how you organize the crew, and how you structure life afloat are what keep people safe and are the most important aspects of safety.

When racing, sometimes you will end up doing things that a normal recreational or cruising sailor wouldn't do. You're pushing the boat harder. You're operating at a more extreme level. And usually you have a more proficient crew on board to back you up. When you do push the boat, even though everybody on board is of the same winning mind-set, you can become complacent. This should never happen. In a race you push your equipment by carrying extra sail area. The bowman does things (such as climbing to the end of the spinnaker pole, or being hoisted to the clew of the spinnaker to change sheets) that, if the guy's mother ever saw him do, she'd never let him go sailing again. But you try to operate with good technique and use the best people on board to do the toughest jobs, so that the person whose life is at risk is in safe hands.

If somebody is getting hauled to the top of the mast to effect a repair, you make sure the person who is most familiar with working the winches is handling the rope that's pulling him up. And the guy who just woke up and is starting his watch on deck isn't the right guy to do that critical task. You put him on the coffee grinder and let him spin the handles to wake up. If it's really rough and the guy up the rig looks like he's going to end up hurting himself, the helmsman should simply bear away—20, 30, 40, 50 degrees off course—for a few seconds, or a minute or two, to effect the repair so the man aloft can get the job done faster and more safely. When you're pushing the boat harder, it takes a higher degree of awareness. There's more responsibility for everybody to look out for the safety of everybody else on the crew.

∽∽∽

Keeping Your Boat Afloat

Dennis Conner always says, "You're not going to win the race if your boat isn't on the finish line." I think back to some of the major breakdowns that boats I've been on have been subjected to. There used to be a big boat series in Hawaii called the Kenwood Cup, and the longest race of that series was the Around the State Race. You started in Oahu and sailed all the way around the western end of the Hawaiian Islands, counterclockwise, then underneath the islands and finally beating up around the backside of the big island of Hawaii. We were winning the race on *Bullfrog*—a 55-foot Doug Peterson design— when in the middle of the night, *bang!* The forestay pulled out of the mast. We were able to jury-rig it, but the breakdown cost us a couple of hours of time—and a podium finish.

It's common sense that boat maintenance is an important part of keeping your boat on the race course. There's maintenance that you should do seasonally or before a big regatta, but there is the daily stuff, too. At the end of a hard day of racing the crew is going to be tired, but it's crucial to go through the full postrace inspection of your boat and your spars. This means grinding a guy up the top of the mast and letting him inspect all the fittings, and having a qualified eye look at all the critical parts on deck and down below. A lot of breakdowns can be avoided with this sort of visual inspection by skilled crew, especially in the common problem areas where the boat and its parts are subjected to chafe or high loads. With experience comes the knowledge of where to look first for signs of damage or wear. It amazes me how often a good sail trimmer will at the end of the day come to me with a written list of things that need attention on the sails. For example, the number-three jib has a small tear in the third batten pocket down, and the mainsail needs work at the luff tape at the half stripe. This sort of attention to detail can mean the difference between winning and losing.

When something *does* break, you should decide whether the problem is in the part that broke (in which case you would upgrade to a stronger part) or some other factor. You don't want to add unnecessary weight to your boat, but it's better to be a little heavy and keep sailing in a race than to be constantly fixing things because your boat is rigged too close to the edge.

When I was in college, a lot of the dinghies we sailed were beginning to succumb to the extra load caused by a new upwind sailing technique—vang sheeting. By pulling on the vang hard on a windy upwind leg, the helmsman could easily pump the mainsail in and out (to keep the boat flat in response to puffs) with the mainsheet without losing the mast bend that kept the mainsail shape nice and flat. With this new technique, however, came a rash of breakdowns—broken booms and broken goosenecks were the first signs that the sailors were putting new stresses on their gear. There was a famous sailor, Jim Miller, who ran a chandlery down on Long Island. He addressed the problem by bringing in a new, heavier aluminum tube for the booms that he sold. Sure, they were heavier than the standard booms. But they stayed together. As Big Jim said, "The boom is a hell of a place to try and save weight."

Maintaining Yourself

At the highest level—whether it's the Olympics or America's Cup or ocean racing—sailing is a very physical sport. And just like for any other athletes, there are sports-specific preparation and exercise routines that the guys and girls at the top level have to go through. No matter whether it's an Olympic sailor who's maintaining his weight and working on core strength so he can hike out harder, or a long-distance ocean sailor who's working on her ability to get by with less sleep in shorter periods so she can handle the watch systems, top sailors must stay in top form.

There is a real benefit in maintaining a good level of general fitness and then focusing on the type of sailing you will be doing. For example, on a big maxi boat you've got to work more on your aerobic and your upper body and grinding strength. There were some grinders in the America's Cup game in the 1980s who got drawn into in the performance-enhancing drug arena, but it wasn't very prevalent then. Today there's virtually none of it. At the America's Cup level, there's random drug testing—they use the same drug testing protocols as the Olympics. For the most part today's America's Cup teams are very health-oriented. Extra strength and speed are important—but so is keeping your crew injury-free—so a lot of the training gets focused on the specific weaknesses of each athlete.

In ocean racing, another focus is on eating well and being generally healthy so you can handle the sleep deprivation that is part of the game. You can see performance slip off when the crew on deck starts nodding off. This is especially common in the early morning hours of the first two nights of a race, before the crew has a chance to settle into the watch system routine. For that reason there are a lot of coffee addicts out there who pump up when they come up on deck. Fortunately coffee is not yet a banned substance in the world of sailboat racing.

When you are part of a rotating watch system in a longer race, it's really important to be able to relax and get to sleep quickly, because you're lucky if you ever get three hours of uninterrupted sleep. One of my tricks is to bring an iPod with foam earplugs that cancel out most of the noise on the boat. When I go off watch, I can tune out and hopefully fall asleep sooner than I would with all the random noise in the boat, which can be incredibly distracting.

I remember a TV show of a Bermuda race where supposedly the navigator on the winning boat didn't sleep at all for the entire three-and-a-half-day race. He just sat at his nav station the entire time and was proud of it. But it was clear that the guy was a complete wreck by the time they finished the race. Don't try to be an iron man!

Sailing on a Wing

In early 2010, for just the second time in America's Cup history, a hard wing-powered multihull won the America's Cup. Larry Ellison's *USA 17* with James Spithill at the helm dominated the *Alinghi* catamaran in two straight races to bring the Cup home again to the United States. But the first Cup victory for a radical wing-sailed boat was in San Diego in 1988, and that victory—over a 135-foot monohull from New Zealand—was even more dominant. I sailed on that catamaran, *Stars & Stripes*, and it was an experience I'll never forget.

But my interest in wing sails goes way back, to my teenage days in Rowayton, Connecticut. It just so happened that at that time a local businessman, Tony DiMauro, had become infatuated with winning the Little America's Cup, a match race in C-class catamarans. The C-class cats were governed by a box rule. As long as your boat fit inside the box, it was legal, so development of rotating masts, fully battened sails, and then semirigid sails started early in that class. By the time I'd moved to Rowayton, teams were testing and racing with fully solid sails, including DiMauro's series of Cup winners named *Patient Lady*. Over the course of my high school years, I was treated to seeing new wing designs regularly, as this was the heyday of the Little America's Cup. I just had to ride my bike down to the Roton Point Beach Club to see these strange foils sitting atop their 25-foot-long, 14-foot-wide catamaran hulls.

So fifteen years later, when it was decided that the *Stars & Stripes* team would defend the Cup in a 60-foot multihull, it was time for me to get reacquainted with the wing. The team brought aboard some of the designers and engineers who had crafted *Patient Lady*'s wing, including the famed Dave Hubbard, and we set out building a three-element wing sail out at aerospace guru Bert Rutan's high-tech aerospace shop, Scaled Composites, in the Mojave desert.

Meanwhile, we built two identical 60-foot catamarans (we had just come off our Cup victory in 1987 with a multiboat campaign, and we strongly believed in the value of using two-boat testing to develop extra speed). But after a month of racing the two boats with traditional rotating masts with fully battened soft sails, our first wing was delivered. It was a masterpiece of engineering, but about 20 percent smaller in area than the soft sail rig that would be the trial horse.

To learn how to sail with a hard wing (you can't just ease the mainsail out until you see it luff to find the optimal angle of attack), we'd put in some time sailing an older *Patient Lady*. During this time we learned to use an innovative telltale device mounted in front of the mast to help set the trim of the wing.

The first day we tested the wing against the soft sail was amazing. Sailing upwind after a rabbit start, the smaller wing was going just fine, about even with the soft sail. But when we tacked, the wing-powered cat jumped forward. A few tacks later, the wing was solidly in the lead. We concluded that the wing tacked better because it had less frictional resistance when the boat was turning through the wind, and it powered up faster than the soft sail. We then rounded a chase boat for a top mark and headed downwind. The wing-sailed catamaran was gone—it was that much faster than the soft-sail-powered cat. Again, the wing's ability to be cambered up by trimming in more depth, and its control of twist, made it much faster downwind—even with less "sail" area. But maybe the most amazing thing about that first day was how easy it was to sail the boat with the wing. All the loads were gone!

The soft sail rig puts a lot more load at points all over the catamaran. Extreme mainsheet tension from a hydraulic ram pulled the aft crossbar upward with immense force. There was no quick retrimming that rig after an ease. And because of the load, the heavily burdened traveler car moved reluctantly. Up forward, that mainsheet load transferred through the sail and straight down the mast, pushing the forward crossbar toward the deep blue sea, requiring a big dolphin striker arrangement underneath the bar.

But with the wing, all the load on the boat seemed to magically disappear. In fact, it was all still being generated, as the boat's speed proved, but it was all transferred elegantly through the solid wing to the mast step—a kind of trailer hitch ball arrangement. There was no mainsheet, just a simple traveler line going straight from a winch on each hull to the "clew" of the wing. You could trim or ease the sail with much less effort and much faster than with the soft sail.

During the next few months, we learned more about trimming the wing, including watching the telltales on the leeward side of the top of the sail to help set the correct trim and twist. Meanwhile, Dennis ordered a new wing—one that was more than 30 percent larger—and it arrived just before the America's Cup. (Sound familiar? BMW Oracle did the same thing again in 2010, upping the size of their solid-wing sail by a huge amount just weeks before the Cup race.)

Another interesting feature of these superfast multihulls is that when sailing downwind, the leading boat can actually send bad air to the trailing boat. The first time I noticed this was happening, I was amazed. But then I did the math, simple high school geometry, and realized that anytime a boat is VMG-ing downwind faster than wind speed it will give bad air to a similarly fast boat trailing it. And the *Stars & Stripes* catamarans were that fast. That is, in moderate winds, if you were to release a helium balloon at the windward mark, just as the cat rounded it, the catamaran would beat that balloon to the leeward mark (although it would have to take an indirect route, jibing downwind)!

As mentioned before, the race against the Kiwis' mega-monohull was a joke. We caned them 2–0 and didn't even need our downwind headsails to do it. It was a chapter that many Cup aficionados lament, but for the crew and designers of *Stars & Stripes*, it was an amazing experience that none will forget—sailing on a boat powered by a wing.

When BMW Oracle mounted their first wing sail in San Diego prior to the 2010 Cup Match, it was déjà vu for me. I talked to team leader Russell Coutts soon thereafter, and it was amazing to hear that their first impressions were exactly the same as ours had been twenty-three years before. The wing rules!

Of course, from a practical standpoint, a wing sail will probably never become commonplace in everyday sailing. This is because it's a bit difficult to hoist and drop the sail every time you want to go sailing. And if you leave the wing up, it's a bit like having a loaded gun—any little puff of wind and that wing will want to jump! But for an America's Cup team, it's the ultimate engine.

～～～

Winning the Cup

My first America's Cup, in Perth, Australia, was incredibly memorable. Not just because it was my first Cup, but also because we *won* it. But the victory kind of snuck up on us. The team had worked hard together for several years. Then the elimination trials took some three and a half months of racing where you're just putting points on the scoreboard. So by the time we got into the semis and then the finals, it was just another day at the office for us.

Every race day we returned to the rough waters off Western Australia and racing *Stars & Stripes*, our America's Cup boat, against the competition. We had a winning record, and over the course of the weeks and months we just kept making small changes to the boat that improved its speed, especially in the breezy conditions. So by the time we faced the Kiwis, who had a better record than we, in the Challenger Finals, we were really peaking at the right time. There have been a few times in my life when I've been close to a sporting team that's peaked at just the right time, and *Stars & Stripes* is one of them.

So we went on and swept the Kiwis, winning 4–1 in that series. When we faced the Aussies in the America's Cup match, it was easy pickings. The Aussies hadn't had the benefit of the incredibly tough trials we had gone through, and the *Kookaburra* team

was no match for the *Stars & Stripes* team. So we won the America's
Cup—just like that. The night we won, some the guys on the
crew called up Jimmy Buffett, who was in town, and invited him
over to the base to play guitar at a little party the crew was having.
I was so tired from the normal daily routine that when it got to
be about nine o'clock, it was my bedtime. I left the base and didn't
even get to see Jimmy play that night at our victory party.

The next morning we woke up and Dennis had a team
meeting (one of the few we had in the entire campaign) where
he told us, "Okay, guys, we're going to be leaving tomorrow on
our own jet. We're going to fly to a White House reception and
then lead a ticker-tape parade down Fifth Avenue in New York."
It was like a dream flying home to the United States with our
crew and families on our own DC-10 with one stop, to clear
customs in Hawaii. I hear that within Continental Airlines, the
legend of the *Stars & Stripes* in-flight victory party still lives. In
San Diego we had a quick parade and then we were off to the
White House, where we got to meet President Bush Sr. in the
Oval Office. It was then off to New York City, where we did
indeed ride down Fifth Avenue in a ticker-tape parade that
Donald Trump threw in honor of the *Stars & Stripes* team.

Meanwhile, Dennis was on the cover of both *Sports
Illustrated* and *Time* in the same week. America's Cup mania
had engulfed America, and ESPN's ratings broke all sorts of
records. For the crew, we had no idea how big our victory was
back home. We had spent the past few months with our heads
down, focused on our job, with few distractions. Then boom!
The whole world seemed to want to be part of our sailing
success. All because we peaked at the right time and did
everything that a sporting team can do to win.

Acknowledgments

It would be impossible to thank everyone who has helped me along the way, or who has taken the time to teach me something new, or who has taken a chance on me as I was rising through the ranks. So to all those not mentioned below, I thank you. However, I would be remiss if I didn't directly acknowledge the following people.

Ted Jones and his family, first for pulling strings to get me into the Norwalk Yacht Club Junior Program, where I got started in my racing, and second for providing a home away from home that was filled to the brim with sailing—from the library to the kitchen.

My mother, who gave free rein to her son as he learned the difference between luff and leech, and started venturing farther and farther afield in his pursuit of sailing nirvana.

The late Tyler Keys for sharing his knowledge of seamanship, navigation, and adventure with a young dreamer who was still looking for traction in his quest to keep sailing while finishing school.

My friends and teammates at Yale Corinthian Yacht Club, and especially my college roommates Steve Benjamin and

Stan Honey, who have each continued to sail at the highest level while pursuing their own unique courses through life.

My Olympic Campaign teammate Dave Perry, whose love for sailing is equaled by his talent as a teacher. Who else can get a group of sailors raucously laughing during a lecture on the driest of subjects: the racing rules?

Dennis Conner—Mr. America's Cup—who, thanks to the recommendation of my longtime friend Tom Whidden (thank you, Tom), was willing to take a chance on a young dinghy sailor to navigate aboard his 12 Meter in his quest to return the Cup to the United States in 1987. Dennis is without question the most talented and focused sailor I've ever raced with, and I was proud to be part of four of his Cup campaigns. I could fill volumes of books with everything I've learned from my years sailing with DC.

My ex-wife JJ Fetter. Thanks to the efforts of her and her teammates (Pam Healy in 1992 and Pease Glaser in 2000), my dream of winning an Olympic medal was vicariously achieved. To be at the Sydney Opera House with our two daughters watching Mom and Pease receive their medals at the medal ceremony was the thrill of a lifetime.

Ricardo Vadia, Brack Duker, Tom and Dottie Hill, and all the sailors who have given me the opportunity to help them prepare and race their boats around the world in some incredible competition.

All the guys and girls with whom I've had the pleasure of racing and sailing over the years. It's a long and ever-growing list of shipmates. I've learned much from many of you and wish fair winds for all your future adventures.

For those who have helped with this book, my friend Peter Economy, who was the catalyst that got this book off the ground, gets first mention. He also provided the inspiration that got me playing guitar in a band . . . but that's a story for another book. Thanks to my editor from John Wiley & Sons, Hana Lane, who saw promise in the concept of this book and brought its publication to fruition. Special thanks to Carmen Hildago, who helped make the cover just exactly perfect. And finally, thanks to my friends and fellow sailors who took the time to share a lesson for this book. Wow, three of them are Olympic gold medalists: Buddy Melges—the Wizard of Zenda—whose penchant for helping others (including me) provided inspiration and a great example that I have tried to emulate. Jonathan McKee, a great friend and one of the most talented sailors I've ever had the pleasure of racing with. We've raced 12 Meters together in the waters off Fremantle, wind-surfed the Columbia River Gorge, and match-raced together off the coast of Tokyo. Each one was a memorable experience. Ben Ainslie, whose enviable record in the one-design and Olympic sailing world is surely just the beginning of a long, successful career in the sport. Ben's focus, drive, and willing-ness to learn even the hardest of lessons are inspirational and I've certainly enjoyed my time on the boat with him and his teams. If they gave gold medals for success in business, George David would have won many indeed. On the water, his sailing campaigns have had much success, most recently with the *Rambler* racing team, which has won races on both sides of the Atlantic (and won races crossing both the North Atlantic and the South Atlantic). Nobody can ask a better question about strategy while sitting on a wet sail in the middle of the night next to the nav station than George. And, finally, thanks to another contributor/Olympic medalist who skippered the boat that broke the longest winning streak in the history of sport: John Bertrand. Since winning the Cup in 1983, John has continued on a course of excellence, breaking new ground in many different fields.

Index